Eternal Life: Ascending Your Soul through The Christian Path

ISBN: 978-1-943392-09-4

Author: Malkut Zedek

Contact: coopertonnn@gmail.com

Table of Contents:

5	The Simple Truth
7	The Word
15	Sexuality
38	Knowledge
48	What Were the Dinosaurs?
81	How to Descend into the 2nd Dimension
87	Heavenly Arithmetic
96	Archetype

The Simple Truth

All Genuine philosophical and spiritual teachings point towards a simple truth: We as Children of the Living God are purposed to inherit a glorious room in His Kingdom[1]. This is not something we should wait for after death, but rather, we should seek this Kingdom within our lifetime[2]. This should not come as a surprise. Why would the Living God require death to initiate you into his Kingdom? Surely, Jesus died **for us**[3], and left us with an open door into His Kingdom that no one can shut[4]. This is found through the straight and narrow path to Life. You are currently dead in your sins[6]. Sin means to miss the mark, or miss the purpose of life. Through repenting, or changing your mind, away from sin, the path is revealed to the Heavenly Kingdom on Earth[7]. Those who will understand and act upon this Word are already written in the Book of Life[8]. Herein is the contents regarding this Born-Again process into the Heavenly Kingdom within your life time – All backed by unabridged scripture. Do not wait; faith without action is dead[9]. The Gift from your Heavenly Father resides in the far reaches of your most glorious imagination[10].

John 11:25-26

> Jesus said to her, "I am the resurrection and the life. The one who believes in me will live, even though they die; and whoever lives by believing in me will never die. Do you believe this?"

1) John 14:2
2) John 11:25-26, John 8:51, Matthew 7:7-8
3) Romans 5:8
4) Revelation 3:8
5) Matthew 7:13-14
6) John 8:21-23
7) John 5:24, Revelation 21:1
8) Revelation 3:5
9) James 2:17
10) Matthew 7:11

The Word

"Everything we call real is made of things that cannot be regarded as real. If quantum mechanics hasn't profoundly shocked you yet, you don't understand it well enough."

-Neils Bohr: Nobel Prize Winner, Father of Quantum Mechanics

To understand the Word of God, you should understand the role of Consciousness in our universe. Quantum physics demonstrated that the conscious observer is integral to the foregoing of our universe. This was confirmed in the double-split experiment.

Electrons are subatomic particles that orbit the nucleus of an atom. An electron can be thought of as a particle, but it also behaves like a wave. When researchers tried to test this dichotomy, they found that the electron behaves like a wave until it is observed. Once it is observed, the waveform collapses into behaving like a particle. This means that the act of observation causes the manifestation of matter. This may seem outlandish, but time and time again this is demonstrated in experimentation. Schrödinger's cat exemplifies this concept. This means that matter could not have given rise to consciousness, as is traditionally thought by secularists. Rather, consciousness is the foundation of our reality.

"I regard consciousness as fundamental. I regard matter as derivative from consciousness. We cannot get behind consciousness. Everything that we talk about, everything that we regard as existing, postulates consciousness."

– Max Planck: Nobel Prize Winner and originator of quantum physics.

Quantum physics comes to a quite simple conclusion: Consciousness is the basis of our reality. With this in mind, we can better understand creation as described in the Gospel of John.

John 1:1-3

"In the beginning was the Word, and the Word was with God, and the Word was God. He was with God in the beginning. Through him all things were made; without him nothing was made that has been made."

This passage indicates consciousness preceded matter. God was (is) an aware entity of pure consciousness. This entity always was and always shall be existent; hence the Alpha-Omega, the beginning and the end. Being pure consciousness, God was able to create things by thinking, and then speaking them into existence. This is the Word. The Greeks call this the Logos, which also means "Reason". This is why John 1 is often referred to as John's Logos. This concept may seem abstract, but it is quite simple; this instant manifestation through thought is what we experience every night in our dreams. In our dreams we think it, and it comes into being. God as Universal Mind is a cornerstone of Judeo-Christian philosophy. God as an all-knowing, all-encompassing Monad of Light (1 John 1:5) and Love (1 John 4:8):

Hebrews 4:13

"Nothing in all creation is hidden from God's sight. Everything is uncovered and laid bare before the eyes of him to whom we must give account."

God is the Universal Author, Source and Cause of all things. God's Light shines within us, and is sought after by those seeking to be children of God. This is precisely the Human Condition that is described in the next section of John's Logos:

John 1:4-13

"In [God] was life, and that life was the light of all mankind. The light shines in the darkness, and the darkness has not overcome it… The true light that gives light to everyone [Jesus] was coming into the world. He was in the world, and though the world was made through him, the world did not recognize him. He came to that which was his own, but his own did not receive him. Yet to all who did receive him, to those who believed in his name, he gave the right to become children of God—children born not of natural descent, nor of human decision or a husband's will, but born of God."

The Mind in all of us, the consciousness that controls the body, the light, is God's Essence that animates our bodies. This is the True Nature within all of us. Our bodily distractions, or sin, casts a veil between us and this light. We can be thought of as conscious appendages of the Almighty conscious Godhead, currently disenchanted by our partial devotion to Mammon, which is the enthrallment with this world. Regardless, we are all participants in this Divine Mind; all is already revealed in the heavenly planes:

Luke 8:7

"For there is nothing hidden that will not be disclosed, and nothing concealed that will not be known or brought out into the open."

We are purposed to see this Truth, but surely we are currently alienated from this Reality. Jesus teaches us how to see this realm which is already in our midst. Our currently dilemma is this:

Mark 4:12

"That seeing they may see, and not perceive; and hearing they may hear, and not understand; lest at any time they should be converted, and their sins should be forgiven them."

God is not the God of dead, but rather, is God of the Living (Luke 20:38). The Living Word of God. We are currently dead in our sin, seeking True perception through the straight and narrow path. Few have found it; neither you nor I have found it – yet. Our integration with God is to be sought in our lifetime. "Seek and you will find, knock and the door will be opened" (Matthew 7:7, Luke 11:9). By following the Word of Truth, we are able to return to our true nature. Our true nature is timeless:

John 8:51-58

> "Very truly I tell you, whoever obeys my word will never see death."

> At this they exclaimed, "Now we know that you are demon-possessed! Abraham died and so did the prophets, yet you say that whoever obeys your word will never taste death. Are you greater than our father Abraham? He died, and so did the prophets. Who do you think you are?"

Through context, we know they are referring to Abraham's physical death, along with the other physical deaths of the prophets. (notice the Pharisee's negligence: Elijah and Enoch both eluded death. Have these traditional members of the Jewish law forgotten scriptures? – Yes) So Jesus replied:

> "… Your father Abraham rejoiced at the thought of seeing my day; he saw it and was glad."

> "You are not yet fifty years old," they said to him, "and you have seen Abraham!"

> "Very truly I tell you," Jesus answered, "before Abraham was born, **I am!**"

Renee Descartes said "I think therefore I am". He was right. When Moses asked God what to call Him, God said to Moses "I am that I am". God is the "I Am", and is the consciousness residing in all of us that gives humans the gift of self-awareness. We as Children inherited this aspect from Our Father. This part of us is immortal, this is why Christ says those who obey his words will not taste death, because their "I Am", their True Being, comes to full expression. This is the "Light of all humankind"; the consciousness within us seeking unity with God's Mind. The Apostles, after following the direction of Christ, found this new Life:

1 John 1:1-6

> "That which was from the beginning, which we have heard, which we have seen with our eyes, which we have looked at and our hands have touched—this we

proclaim concerning the Word of life. The life appeared; we have seen it and testify to it, and we proclaim to you the eternal life, which was with the Father and has appeared to us. We proclaim to you what we have seen and heard, so that you also may have fellowship with us. And our fellowship is with the Father and with his Son, Jesus Christ. We write this to make our joy complete. This is the message we have heard from him and declare to you: God is light..."

Light as consciousness makes sense when analyzing the neuroanatomy of various brain structures. The pineal gland, located deep within the brain, has been theorized to be the seat of the soul; the gateway between spirit and matter. Despite being located deep within the skull and isolated from external light, the pineal gland has an abundance of photoreceptors, which are purposed for responding to light. Why does the pineal gland have photoreceptors if it is never exposed to light outside the body? It can be likened to the control stick for God's Consciousness (Light). It is the place where "I Am" interfaces with the body. This is why the pineal gland, the 3rd eye, is to be purified to allow God's Light consciousness to shine through it. The pineal gland has been deemed "the 3rd eye" because it visualizes Spirit:

Matthew 6:22

"The lamp of the body is the **eye**, if, therefore, thine **eye** may be perfect, all thy body shall be enlightened,"

Notice how eye is singular here? This is a direct reference to the pineal gland, the single eye within the brain. When your spiritual essence becomes perfected, God becomes fully manifest in your awareness. Once sin is omitted from your being, your True Light shines. To sin simply means "to miss the mark"; by sinning we are missing the point of life; by omitting sin true life is revealed. This causes a transcendental transformation into the light, as demonstrated by Jesus' Transfiguration:

Matthew 17:1-2

"And after six days Jesus taketh Peter, and James, and John his brother, and doth bring them up to a high mount by themselves, and he was transfigured before them, and his face shone as the sun, and his garments did become white as the light..."

The neuroanatomical substrate for this transformation is the pineal gland; this is the "place" where we commune with God's Mind.

Genesis 32:30

> And Jacob calleth the name of the place **Peniel** (pronounced pineal): **for `I have seen God face unto face, and my life is delivered;'**

All Jesus's commands, as well as the other legitimate prophets, are purposed for perfecting the soul which allows your inner eye to shine bright to enlightenment.

Matthew 7:3-5

> "Why do you look at the speck of sawdust in your brother's eye and pay no attention to the plank in your own **eye**? How can you say to your brother, 'Let me take the speck out of your eye,' when all the time there is a plank in your own eye? You hypocrite, first take the plank out of your own **eye**, and then you will see clearly to remove the speck from your brother's eye."

This is a very important concept that few take to heart. Do not worry about fixing the world, or fixing others, rather, fix yourself first, and then you will be able to fix the world. This has magnificent implications. Upon fixing your inner state of mind, and thus purifying the soul, the exterior world follows suite. In Hindu tradition, this is Atman (self) realization of its connection with Brahman (outside world). This is because the same Soul that manifests the inside, also manifest the outside:

Matthew 23: 25-26

> "Woe to you, teachers of the law and Pharisees, you hypocrites! You clean the outside of the cup and dish, but inside they are full of greed and self-indulgence. Blind Pharisee! First clean the inside of the cup and dish, and then the outside also will be clean."

This means that upon perfecting your inner self, your body and the world will follow suite. So many of us are so preoccupied with finding the beam (imperfection) in the eye (pineal gland – soul) of others, that we are blind to our own imperfect actions. You reap what you sow. The actions you do, and the beliefs you hold, will manifest as external reality. This is why you should do to others what you would have done to you:

Matthew 7:12

> "So in everything, do to others what you would have them do to you, for this sums up the Law and the Prophets."

Hindu tradition calls this "Karma", in physics this is Newton's 3rd Law of nature: "For every action, there is an equal and opposite reaction". By sinning, you are unveiling a tree of bad fruit and thus karmic consequence. Christ buffered, and ended, the endless karmic feedback loop that was generated by the first sin in the garden. He did this by taking such a heinous punishment despite not deserving any malice.

Roman 5:8

"But God commendeth his love toward us, in that, while we were yet sinners, **Christ died for us.**"

Christ literally died **for us**. Many say this without understanding the deeper implications. Jesus was the ultimate sacrifice; the perfect firstborn of God to atone for the sins of all humankind. In the Old Testament, the Israelites would sacrifice their firstborn livestock to attenuate their sin. Now, Jesus was and is the ultimate sacrifice that gives us an open door into the Kingdom (Revelation 3:8). This is open door is made clear to those who are diligent on the straight and narrow path; once they find the door, they knock, and it is opened.

The disobedient things you do manifest consequently in the external world and are presented to you through various circumstances. This is purposed for discipline of your soul. If you become adept at reading the present moment, you can begin to see the karmic feedback you are receiving, or the fruit you are yielding, and you can discern the current condition of your soul:

Luke 12:54-57

"When you see a cloud rising in the west, immediately you say, 'It's going to rain,' and it does. And when the south wind blows, you say, 'It's going to be hot,' and it is. Hypocrites! You know how to interpret the appearance of the earth and the sky. **How is it that you don't know how to interpret this present time?** Why don't you judge for yourselves what is right?"

The Spirit is constantly trying to bring your soul towards God's Presence (Kingdom). It does so by manifesting the condition of your soul through circumstantial situations in the present moment. This is your present condition, deemed Purgatory. When you are interacting with other people, take note to the actions they do that you find distasteful. **This is a symbolic representation of the same distasteful traits you possess.** It's quite poetic, and is reminiscent of the words of Shakespeare:

"All the world's a stage,
And all the men and women merely players"

This is why reality is often expressed in a seemingly poetic form. God's Word is the foundation for the entire poetic epic of human history. His plan was revealed by the meaning of the names of the children after Adam:

www.bible-codes.org

When the meanings of these names are read in succession, we see God's plan to redeem the world with the death of his Son Jesus (Jesus is referred to as the Glory of God – 2 Corinthians: 4-6). This was all presupposed and indicated by the names of Christ's lineage, based on God's Word of Truth, long ago. Reading the meaning of the names from Adam to Noah also extends all the way through Jesus's lineage and expresses a more detailed description of God's intent for humanity. This immense depth of detail demonstrates a consistent author throughout the text – God. This full description is laid out on www.bible-codes.org. This is also why the people in the Old Testament named their children after the scenario in which they were born – this was showing the intimate connection of the poetic God Mind with the lower material plane. This is a demonstration of the poetic and symbolic aspect of reality. Reality manifests in its grossest form as matter, whereas symbolic concepts simultaneously manifest on a higher plane and speak to the soul. This is why Jesus taught in parables – the truth was best articulated on the symbolic spiritual plane.

Judge for yourself what is right, and truly analyze yourself and you will see that this is the case. The external world is the fruit that you are yielding. All Good trees yield Good fruit, and all bad trees yield bad fruit. This is how you can tell your soul's condition; what sort of fruit do you bear?

Matthew 12:33-35

> "Make a tree good and its fruit will be good, or make a tree bad and its fruit will be bad, for a tree is recognized by its fruit. You brood of vipers, how can you who are evil say anything good? For the mouth speaks what the heart is full of. A good man brings good things out of the good stored up in him, and an evil man brings evil things out of the evil stored up in him."

Your word is an expression of your heart. If you fasten your word to God's Word, which is Truth, Love and Light, you will commune with God. Currently you live according to your own volition, the tempter's volition. You are acting – your True self, which resides in Christ, is yearning for liberation. The Good seed is so often strangled by the anxieties of this world. When we submit all of our reliance to God's plan, we begin the assimilation process. Jesus is God's Word manifest in the flesh, purposed to gather the lost sheep.

John 1:14

> "The Word became flesh and made his dwelling among us. We have seen his glory, the glory of the one and only Son, who came from the Father, full of grace and truth."

Jesus was (is) God's Word in flesh, and came to teach us to return to our intended paradise in God's Mind, in which there are many spiritual "mansions" (John 14:2). In order to understand where the soul is headed, it is important to first understand from where humanity came.

Sexuality

In nature, every particle has an anti-particle; every substance has an equal and opposite particle: the proton and the anti-proton, the electron and the anti-electron, etc. Humanity is no exception to this rule. Male and female fits this law. These two states are often represented by – and +. Then there is the neutral 0, which is the union of the two. Similarly, there is male, female, and the union of the two. This is clearly expressed in Genesis. Humanity began as a unified Entity. Humanity was made in the image of Elohim:

Genesis 1:26

"Then Elohim said, 'Let us make humans in **our** image, in **our** likeness.' "

Notice the plurality of Elohim. Humanity was made in Their image. Elohim is a combination of two words: El and Eloah. El means God, and Eloah means Goddess, and the word is plural. Altogether, Elohim therefore means "Gods and Goddesses". The original human was manifest as Adam. But, this is a little confusing. If the first human was made in the image of Elohim, or "Gods and Goddesses", it would have by nature been the United form of Male and Female. This was clearly stated in Genesis:

Genesis 1:27

"And Elohim prepareth the man in Their image… **a male and a female** They prepared Them."

Genesis 5:1-2

"In the day of God's preparing man, in the likeness of God He hath made him; **a male and a female He hath prepared them**, and He blesseth them, and calleth **their** name Man, in the day of their being prepared."

Elohim is not synonymous with the "The Most High God", that Jesus calls his Father. This Most High God, called "Ruach Elohim", among other names, in Genesis 1:1 is the chief Creator. Therefore, Elohim, which were created by the Most High God, are arbitrators of creation, like a communion of angels. Before the fall, Adam/Eve had domain over the creation, and did not require work in the conventional sense. They did not undergo the stresses we experience today, everything was in perfect coordination. Then something happened that would lead to the fall of Humanity; the Human was separated into male and female form, so that they could experience companionship.

Genesis 2:18

> "And Jehovah God saith, `Not good for the man to be alone, I do make to him an helper -- as his counterpart.' "

In the verse before this, God gave a warning:

Genesis 2:17

> "...of the tree of knowledge of good and evil, thou dost not eat of it, for in the day of thine eating of it -- dying thou dost die."

Understanding the tree of knowledge of good and evil is key to ascertaining our current condition. God gave this decree immediately after separating the human into male and female. Therefore, we can conclude that separating the human into Male and Female forms led to the possibility of eating from the Tree of Knowledge, and perhaps free will in general.

There were two trees in the **middle** of the garden: The Tree of life, and the Tree of knowledge of good and evil (Genesis 2:9). Both were in the midst of the "Garden", which is the Human body. The trees in the middle of our body is a reference to the spinal cord.

The autonomic nervous system is responsible for bodily functions that do not require our conscious input, such as our heartbeat. The autonomic nervous system is mostly located in our spine, in the **midst** of our body. The autonomic nervous system is considered the "reptilian brain", because these are the dominant structures present in a reptile's brain

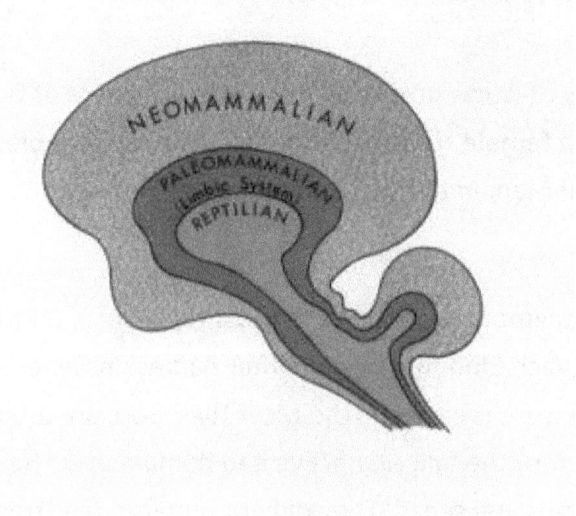

The reptilian brain is divided into two sub-categories: The Sympathetic Nervous System (SNS) and the Parasympathetic Nervous System (PNS). The PNS is responsible for rest and

repair, and is vital to maintain the healthy human body. The SNS is responsible for fight or flight reflex, or in other words, coping with stressful situations. When one of these systems becomes more active, it causes the other to become less active, and vice versa.

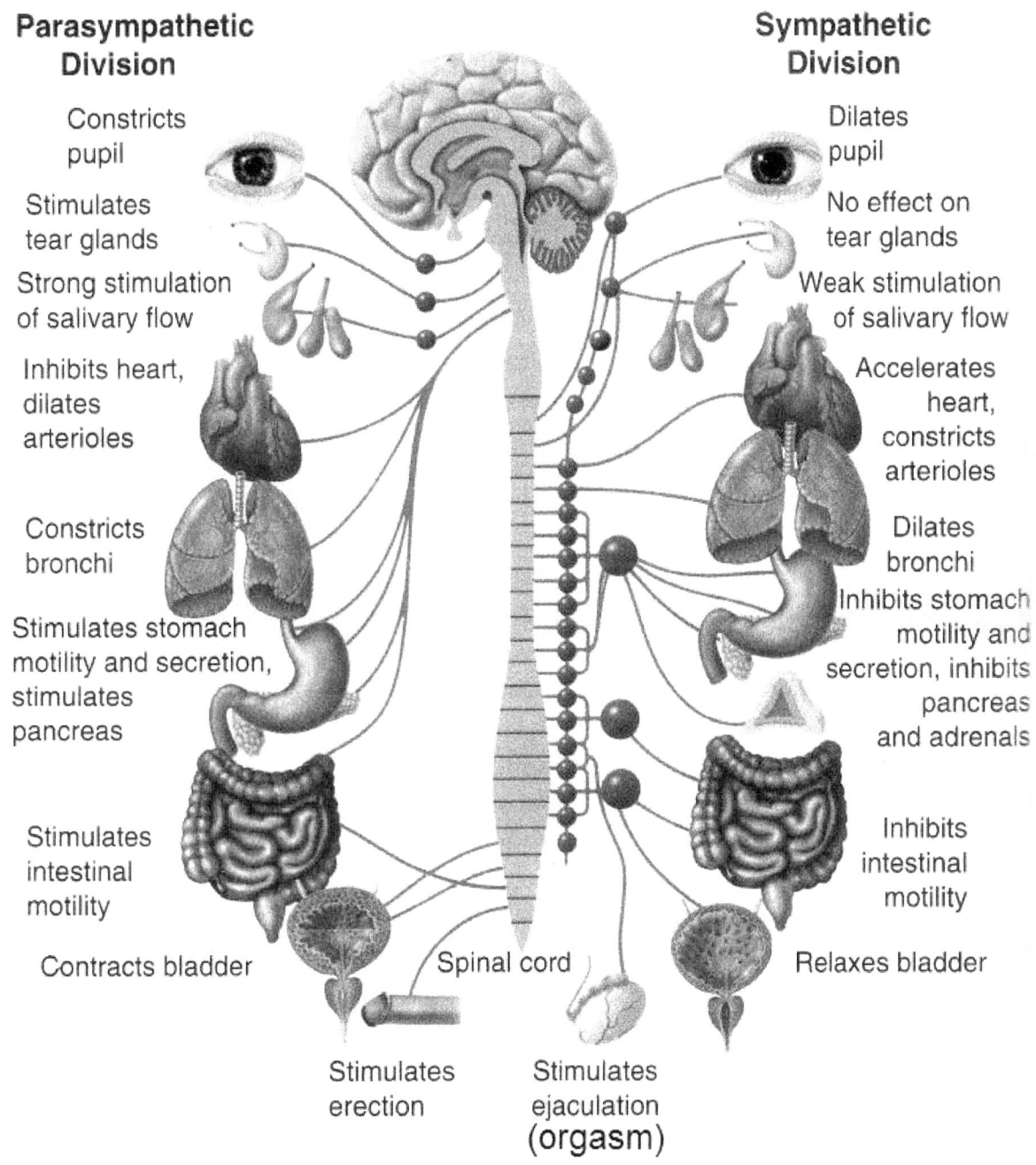

The reptilian brain is manifest as the serpent in Genesis 3. The two trees in the midst of the Garden are the PNS and SNS of this reptilian brain located in the spine in the midst of our body. The PNS is the tree of life, because it perpetuates healing. The SNS is the tree of knowledge of good and evil, because it copes with stressful scenarios.

When Adam and Eve activated the SNS, or ate of the tree of knowledge of good and evil, they were surely to die. This is because the SNS causes the release of stress hormones to cope with stressful stimuli, but these same hormones cause bodily malfunction as a side-effect. It is well known by neurologists that activating the SNS lowers the expression of the PNS, and vice versa. Because they activated the SNS, the PNS would no longer work perfectly, and without a perfect repair system they were no longer immortal:

Genesis 3:22

> "And Jehovah God saith, `Lo, the man was as one of Us, as to the knowledge of good and evil (SNS); and now, lest he send forth his hand, and have taken also of the tree of life (PNS), and eaten, and lived eternally,' "

It is interesting how the author(s) of Genesis was capable of grasping the immense complexity of these neural systems without the medical diagnostic tools and methods available today. In history, this dichotomy is present in the caduceus, a symbol commonly seen in medical institutions. The caduceus is most commonly associated with Hermes, the supposed messenger of God.

Notice the two snakes representing the PNS and SNS subdivisions of the reptilian brain coiled around a spinal column. At the top is a pinecone-looking structure, this is the pineal gland which is located on top of the spine. This is also evident in the staff of Osiris:

    This is also the integral theme in Jewish Kabbalah, which roots its ideologies in the Tree of Life. It is no coincidence that the layout of the Kabbalistic Tree of Life is in the exact form of the anatomy of the spine which contains the tree of life. The ganglionic extensions of the spine form the side branches of the Kabbalistic tree of life. Because the ancients were so in-tuned with creation, they based their traditions off human anatomy because it is integral to the creative act of human Genesis. The crown is at the top, representative of the cerebral cortex which literally crowns the nervous system. At the base is the root of the tree, which is representative of the cauda equina, which means "horse's tail" and looks like a tree root. This is also the basis of the chakra energy centers, which is discussed in more detail later.

Kabbalah Tree of Life

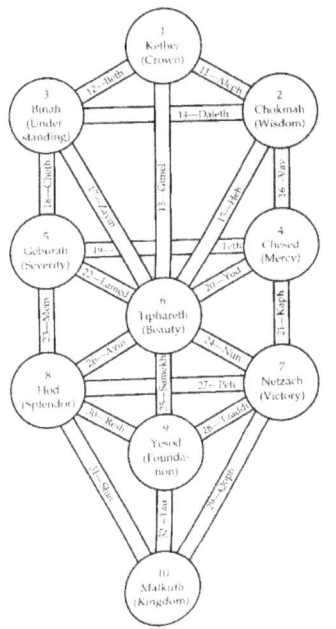

Spine Anatomy: Tree of Life with Ganglionic Branches

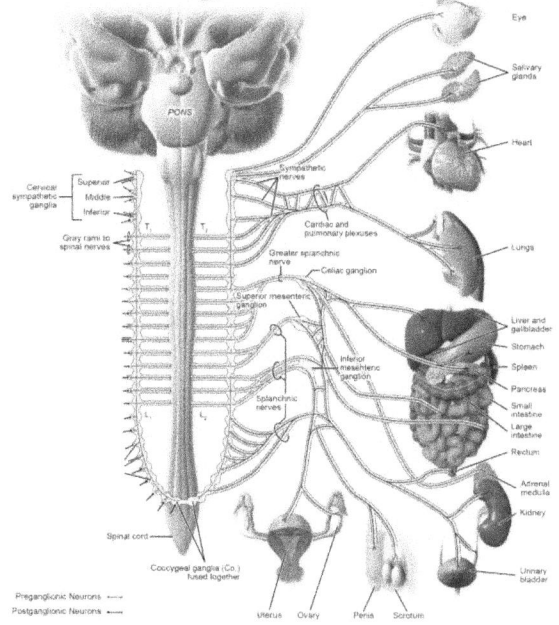

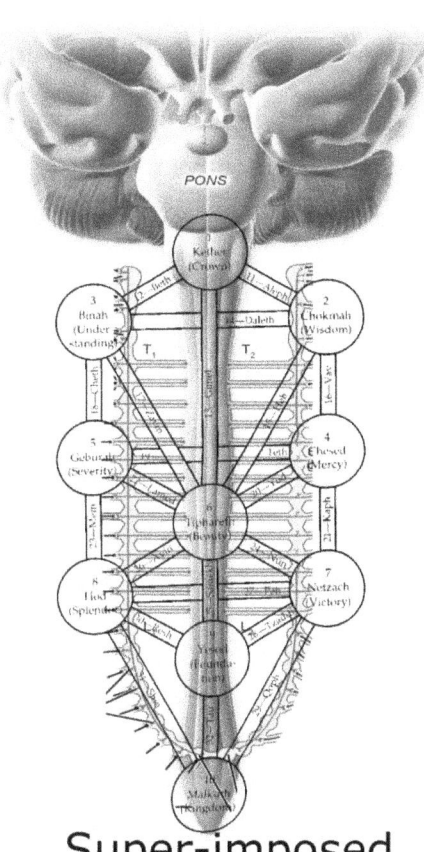

Super-imposed

So, what exactly did they do that activated the SNS, which is the Tree of Knowledge? When they were separated into male and female in Genesis 2:18, God made the decree not to eat the fruit of the SNS. This is a reference to the orgasm. It is also important to note that fruit is the sexual organ of the plant. The orgasm, along with all the other happenings afterwards, are all hallmarks of the SNS:

Pupil Dilation – "Their eyes were opened…" (Genesis 3:7)

Fear and Hiding – "…the man and his wife hide themselves from… Jehovah God…" (Genesis 3:8, 10)

Conventional Childbirth (Made Possible by the Male Orgasm) – (Genesis 3:16)

Stressful Work and General Survival – (Gen 3:17, 19, 21, 23)

In the Bible, to "know" is sometimes synonymous with the orgasm/child-birth. This is evident in Genesis 4:

Genesis 4:1

> "And the man **knew** Eve his wife, and she conceiveth and beareth Cain, and saith, `I have gotten a man by Jehovah;' "

Genesis 4:17

> "and Cain **know**eth his wife, and she conceiveth, and beareth Enoch; and he is building a city, and he calleth the name of the city, according to the name of his son -- Enoch."

Genesis 4:25

> "And Adam again **know**eth his wife, and she beareth a son, and calleth his name Seth, `for God hath appointed for me another seed instead of Abel:' for Cain had slain him."

To "know", often means conception. The orgasm, which resulted in childbirth, opened up the legendary Pandora's Box, activating the SNS and introducing decay to a once-perfect Humankind. Think about it, for perfect human beings, procreation is not required, because death did not occur. Now that death came, children were required to forego humankind. This was the double entendre of this act. It is important to note that the erection is not activated by the SNS, but rather, is part of the PNS. This means that prior to the orgasm, they were unified in a blissful state of connection. Intercourse **without male orgasm** is non-depletive, and allows the eternal bliss that Adam and Eve experienced prior to Adam's orgasm. This is the root of tantric sex and the purpose of the missionary position. The male orgasm is depletive, this is why it was only once Adam ate of the "tree of knowledge" that humanity was cursed. Eve's orgasm had no consequences, except the fact that it lured Adam to do the same.

This comprehensive account of the autonomic nervous system, the reptilian brain, and its intricate workings given to us by the author(s) of Genesis clearly demonstrate that these writings were divinely inspired. Now that contemporary medical knowledge has caught up to the wisdom in this Holy text, we can finally disambiguate the meaning of our history. This also makes sense as to why Jesus was born the way he was. The birth of Christ demonstrates the redemptive aspect of giving birth to a child without the husband "knowing" his wife:

Luke 1:30-35

> And the messenger said to her, `Fear not, Mary, for thou hast found favour with God; and lo, thou shalt conceive in the womb, and shalt bring forth a son, and call his name Jesus..." And Mary said unto the messenger, `How shall this be, **seeing a husband I do not know?**' And the messenger answering said to her, `The Holy Spirit shall come upon thee, and the power of the Highest shall overshadow thee, therefore also the holy-begotten thing shall be called Son of God;"

This is the great Redemption, the New Adam who would atone for all the wrong-doings of humankind and thus dispel the curse. This is God's new creation, with Him as the unadulterated Father. By doing this, Jesus reconciled the enmity caused by Adam and Eve (Genesis 3:15) and reopened the possibility of the Sacred Union of Male and Female.

As Humanity left paradise as a couple, it seems as though in this age we are purposed to re-enter paradise as a couple, reobtaining the unionized bliss experienced by Adam and Eve before the orgasm:

Mark 10:7-8
> "...on this account shall a man leave his father and mother, and shall cleave unto his wife, **and they shall be -- the two -- for one flesh; so that they are no more two, but one flesh**"

Jesus is directly referencing this Holy Union that repositions the two into Holy Bliss. The Sacred Embrace, the Holy of Holies. Intercourse without male orgasm is called Karezza which is deeply rooted in transcendental traditions. This is likely what is being eluded to in the story of Noah: They entered the "Ark" *two-by-two*. The substance that the "Ark" is made from is completely untranslatable and is never used again in the rest of the Bible. Surely this is some sort of spiritual vessel which cannot be explained in conventional writing. From this Covenant came the pure seed from which Humankind would start anew.

Jesus references this Sacred Union when talking to the woman at the well. The Gift of God is this; Eternal Bliss with the spiritual counterpart:

John 4:10-16
> Jesus answered her, "If you knew the **gift of God** and who it is that asks you for a drink, you would have asked him and he would have given you living water...Everyone who drinks this water will be thirsty again, but... the water I give them will become in them a spring of water welling up to **eternal life**."
>
> The woman said to him, "Sir, give me this water so that I won't get thirsty and have to keep coming here to draw water."
>
> He told her, "Go, **call your husband** and come back."

When the woman at the well asks how to receive the gift of God and eternal life, Jesus tells her to find her husband. This is the Sacred Embrace; the return to Eden and higher. Unfortunately for the woman, all her "husbands" thus far have been karmic manifestations; relationships that were indicative of her deficient soul. Many settle for a mate that is not their soul counterpart. This occurs due to sin, or "missing the mark", which deviates us from the Divine Plan. By understanding yourself, and living according to truth, your True counterpart is introduced:

John 4:17-18

> "I have no husband," she replied.
>
> Jesus said to her, "You are right when you say you have no husband. The fact is, you have had five husbands, and the man you now have is not your husband. What you have just said is quite true."

None of the woman's current or past "husbands" were her true Husband. Therefore, she was incapable of tapping into the well of eternal life. This mystery is expounded upon in the Gospel of Phillip, which is a text that was found in Nag Hammadi in the mid 20th century.

This sacred Union is discussed in all beliefs and philosophies that have discerned Truth, such as the Greeks. In Dante's Inferno, he claimed that the Greeks, in all their knowledge, were in a state of limbo. They had attained the knowledge of Christ, but because of their lack of belief/action, they were incapable of entering the Holy City. In various Greek manuscripts this knowledge is evident. Aristophanes talks to Plato about the purpose of love, and reunion with the soul's mate:

Plato's Symposium

> "...human nature was originally one and we were a whole, and the desire and pursuit of the whole is called love. There was a time, I say, when we were one, but now because of the wickedness of mankind God has dispersed us... And if we are not obedient to the gods, there is a danger that we shall remain split... Wherefore let us exhort all men to piety in all things, that we may avoid evil and obtain the good, taking Love for our leader and commander.
>
> Let no one oppose him--he is the enemy of the gods who opposes him. For if we are friends of God and at peace with him we shall find our own true loves, which rarely happens in this world at present. I am serious... my words have a wider application -they include men and women everywhere; and I believe that if our loves were perfectly accomplished, and each one returning to his primeval nature had his original true love, then our race would be happy. And if this would be best of all, the best in the next degree must in present circumstances be the nearest approach to such a union; and that will be the attainment of a congenial love.
>
> Wherefore, if we would praise him who has given to us the benefit, we must praise the god Love ("God is Love" [1 John 4:8]), who is our greatest benefactor, both leading us in this life back to our own nature, and giving us high hopes for

the future, for he promises that if we are pious, he will restore us to our original state, and heal us and make us happy and blessed."

If this is true, why does Paul say it is better to not marry? It is obvious that God's Truth should be on the forefront of our motives, and marriage could be a distraction and prevent us from reaching complete Truth in Christ. This command to not marry is purposed to prevent us from falling into this trap. It was not like this from the beginning, in which humanity lived in a state of union, expressed by Adam and Eve prior to their fall:

Matthew 19:3-12

> " And the Pharisees came near to him, tempting him, and saying to him, `Is it lawful for a man to put away his wife for every cause?'
>
> And he answering said to them, `Did ye not read, that He who made [them], from the beginning a male and a female made them,
>
> and said, For this cause shall a man leave father and mother, and cleave to his wife, and they shall be -- the two -- for one flesh?
>
> so that they are no more two, but one flesh; what therefore God did join together, let no man put asunder.'
>
> They say to him, `Why then did Moses command to give a roll of divorce, and to put her away?'
>
> He saith to them -- `Moses for your stiffness of heart did suffer you to put away your wives, but from the beginning it hath not been so.
>
> `And I say to you, that, whoever may put away his wife, if not for whoredom, and may marry another, doth commit adultery; and he who did marry her that hath been put away, doth commit adultery.'
>
> His disciples say to him, `If the case of the man with the woman is so, it is not good to marry.'
>
> And he said to them, `All do not receive this word, but those to whom it hath been given; for there are eunuchs who from the mother's womb were so born; and there are eunuchs who were made eunuchs by men; and there are eunuchs

who kept themselves eunuchs because of the reign of the heavens: he who is able to receive [it] -- let him receive.'"

Here we see clearly that Jesus endorses marriage, and thus the reuniting of the flesh, while at the same time realizes that false marriages, through hardened hearts, has detracted many from Christ life. Marriage, indicated by Jesus talking to the woman at the well, is God's Gift to us in our current state. Once Truth is revealed in the Great Revelation, we will no longer be given up in marriage, but will be as the angels communing with God for all eternity (Matthew 22:30). This is the unified state not just of man and woman, but of all humankind within God's Mind which we receive our apportioned "Mansion" (John 14:2).

Our original state was most expressed when we were children. We loved without the adulteration of lustful thoughts. Once we go through maturity, and our hormones allow sexual activity, we are often led astray by impure sexual thoughts and behavior. This is one of the many reasons why Jesus insists we look through the eyes of a child. Their minds are untainted by sexual aberration. Seeking our original state, our original Love, involves dismantling our lustful impurity:

Revelation 2:1-7

To the angel of the church in Ephesus write:

These are the words of him who holds the seven stars in his right hand and walks among the seven golden lampstands. I know your deeds, your hard work and your perseverance. I know that you cannot tolerate wicked people, that you have tested those who claim to be apostles but are not, and have found them false. You have persevered and have endured hardships for my name, and have not grown weary.

Yet I hold this against you: You have forsaken the love you had at first. Consider how far you have fallen! Repent and do the things you did at first. If you do not repent, I will come to you and remove your lampstand from its place. But you have this in your favor: You hate the practices of the Nicolaitans (Men of power), which I also hate.

He who is having an ear -- let him hear what the Spirit saith to the assemblies: To him who is overcoming **-- I will give to him to eat of the tree of life that is in the midst of the paradise of God.**

Jesus' teachings lead us back to the tree of life (PNS) which Adam and Eve were alienated from due to tapping into the tree of knowledge (SNS). This is why all of Jesus's teachings involve silencing the sympathetic nervous system (SNS), and thus activating the parasympathetic nervous system (PNS - Tree of Life). Making your burden light, dropping your nets, devoting yourself to unconditional loving kindness, serving God and not money, and humility are all ways to bring the Tree of Life to expression. By putting faith in God's intent, your survival mechanisms (SNS) are quieted, allowing the grace of the Tree of Life to flow through your Being. This will Redeem the first love and attract the Soul's Mate and lead to the unionized, blissful state that is prevalent in Christian-based art throughout history, which eludes to the Sacred Union:

Notice that the androgyne, the spiritually unionized male and female, is standing above a serpent. This is indicative of their triumph over material lust, and resolving the fall of humankind. In Christian alchemical lore, this is called "Taming the beast", which means to tame the carnal desires. This is why adultery, a beastly desire, is condemned; it prevents the Sacred Embrace. Also notice the crown; they have becomes Masters, and have achieved Life that few people find (Revelation 2:10). The sun and moon are representative of the dual nature of the cosmos which is reflected in the dual nature of the human. This teaching is also seen in Hindu tradition:

The Unionized Male-Female God is common throughout Hindu tradition. Sadhguru expounds on this mystery:

Ardhanarishvara – When the Ultimate Man Became Half-Woman

> "Generally Shiva is referred to as the ultimate man, he is the symbolism of ultimate masculinity, but you will see in the Ardhanarishvara (pictures above on the right) form of Shiva, one half of him is a fully developed woman. Let me tell you the story of what happened. Shiva was in an ecstatic condition and because

of that, Parvati was drawn to him. After Parvati did many things to woo him and sought all kinds of help, they got married. Once they were married, naturally, Shiva wanted to share whatever was his experience. Parvati said, "This state that you are in within yourself, I want to experience it too. What should I do? Tell me. I am willing to do any kind of austerity." Shiva smiled and said, "There is no need for you to do any great austerity. You just come and sit on my lap." Parvati came and with absolutely no resistance towards him, sat on his left lap. Since she was so willing, since she had placed herself totally in his hands, he just pulled her in and she became half of him.

You need to understand, if he has to accommodate her in his own body, he has to shed half of himself. So he shed half of himself and included her. This is the story of Ardhanarishvara. This is basically trying to manifest that the masculine and the feminine are equally divided within yourself. And when he included her, he became ecstatic. What is being said is that if the inner masculine and feminine meet, you are in a perpetual state of ecstasy. If you try to do it on the outside, it never lasts, and all the troubles that come with that are an ongoing drama.

Essentially, it is not two people longing to meet, it is two dimensions of life longing to meet – outside as well as inside. If you achieve it inside, the outside will happen one hundred percent by choice. If you do not achieve it inside, the outside will be a terrible compulsion. This is the way of life."

Take the bolded portion above to heart; the outwardly desire to find a mate is a compulsion, whereas finding your true self will effortlessly and naturally attract your Companion. Likewise, do not enthrall yourself with the pursuit of a wife, but rather, with the pursuit of God, and he will happily give you your Beloved.

Proverbs 18:20

"He who finds a wife finds a good thing and obtains favor from the Lord."

The story of Ardhanarishvara is exactly like the Christian tradition. It insists that by finding perfect balance within, the outside world will follow suit. Upon cleaning the inside of the cup, the outside of the cup will follow (Matthew 23:26). Observing your true feelings towards your biological mother and father reveals your inner dual nature. You will see traits in your parents that you find distasteful; this is indicative of your inner male-female imbalance. By observing these traits in your parents, you can fix them in yourself and break the chain of sin being passed on through the generations. This is the underlying meaning of "honoring your father and mother"; balancing your male and female aspects. The sort of balance described here results in the presentment of the kingdom of God. This sort of balance is also indicated in our neuroanatomy.

The pineal gland resides between the two cerebral hemispheres of the brain. The pineal gland is responsible for DMT release. DMT, dimethyltryptamine, is the neurochemical which has been strongly correlated to cognitive upliftment in which people "see" the notion of unconditional loving kindness with an intense light that they can only explain as the presence of God. DMT can be thought of as the natural chemical neurotransmitter of spirit which intensifies with a properly functioning pineal gland. Jesus teaches us how to purify our "eye", and fully activate this through baptism which allows the born again faculty of Spirit to enter the frontier of God's Kingdom within us. This is the reason for the following passage:

Genesis 32:30

> "And Jacob calleth the name of the place **Peniel** (pronounced pineal): for `I have seen God face unto face, and my life is delivered;'"

This has also been verified by scientific report. According to the study 'A sideways look at the Neurobiology of Psi', the pineal gland is responsible for "The mediation of spontaneous mystical and visionary states...". Jesus, as well as other legitimate prophets, have given teachings that facilitate a properly functioning tree of life and pineal gland which results in miraculous fruit. This allows our inner vision to become in-tune with Divinity.

The Male-Female dichotomy also manifests in the higher realm. This is consistent on all heavenly and earth planes. You often hear that the Christian God is the Father. The Most High God is male because it was the source of the original emanations of Spirit, whereas the Heavenly Mother was the receptive aspect to these emanations. This is why it is called "Mother Earth", and is also why when the Father inserted his spirit into the dust (Mother) that the human being was made.

Genesis 2:7

> "And Jehovah God formeth the man -- dust from the ground, and breatheth into his nostrils breath of life, and the man becometh a living creature."

Matthew 3:9

> "...I tell you that out of these stones God can raise up children..."

Matter in general is the Feminine aspect of creation, whereas Spirit is Male. The Latin word mater, which means mother, is the basis for the word matter. Our bodies, in terms of Heavenly Gender roles, are feminine. This is why Isaiah calls the people of God "Daughters of Zion". Our bodies, mater, are the feminine aspect of creation, and we are currently seeking fulfilment from the Spirit of the Heavenly Father in this lifetime. This is the Heavenly marriage which Jesus calls "The Bride-Chamber":

Mark 2:19-20

> And Jesus said to them, `Are the sons of the bride-chamber able, while the bridegroom is with them, to fast? so long time as they have the bridegroom with them they are not able to fast; but days shall come when the bridegroom may be taken from them, and then they shall fast -- in those days.

Jesus is the bridegroom, the Heavenly Male aspect of Spirit being introduced to humankind. Fasting hastens the coming of the Bridegroom, but is no longer useful when the Heavenly Marriage has occurred within you. This internal marriage coincides with the outer marriage and the realization of your earthly Spouse. The Jewish people in the Old Testament were awaiting the coming of this Male aspect which was alienated from humankind due to sin. They always had their Heavenly Mother, which is their body and matter in general. This is exemplified by the birth of Jesus. The Heavenly Father impregnates Matter (Jesus's mother) with the Spirit:

Matthew 1:18

> "And of Jesus Christ, the birth was thus: For his mother Mary having been betrothed to Joseph, before their coming together she was found to have conceived from the Holy Spirit,"

Our entire 3-dimensional existence can be referred to as the 3D matrix. Matrix, also derived from "mater", means breeding woman. This is the place in which the Spirit is born; Jesus calls this our second birth. We are currently in the motherly womb, the matrix, and like Neo from the movie, we are seeking liberation into the limitless realm of Spirit. Likewise,

Socrates claims we are currently in a state of becoming, seeking a permanent state of being. This state of being is the present form of the verb to be – "I Am"; which is God.

When Jesus went into the wilderness for 40 days he was being born again in the womb of the Earthly Mother. Jesus did not require such purification, but did this to demonstrate for us the way. Through purifying your earthly faculties, we are born again into the realm of spirit in our Father's Kingdom. Fasting brings upon the Bridegroom, the Heavenly Male aspect, into the Bride-Chamber within you. This is why Jesus, during his fast, was tempted with rulership of the world; he was a complete Spiritual master and it rendered him with infinite material prowess. This is why he says nothing will be impossible for us – once the born again process is complete (Matthew 17:20). He follows this statement by saying prayer and fasting will facilitate this process. The adversary tempts the humble Jesus, but he does not fall for such temptation, because he knows the realm of Spirit is 100 times greater than any material splendor. Similarly, Buddha was tempted by Mara the demon prior to his enlightenment. He was tempted by beautiful seductresses which Mara was working through.

As is our ascent; seductresses which lure you away from the straight and narrow path are an indication that you are well on your way to being born again – which is self-realization. In Islamic tradition, these beautiful men/women (depending on your gender) are called houris. These houris begin to appear as your life is devoted to Truth – God. These houris are defined as jewel-eyed, pure, well-matched men/women who are of similar age. This can be simplified to the law of Love attracting a likewise mate into your life. This aspect of life arises when nearing paradise. Diotima, when talking with Socrates, describes this phenomenon of the upward ascent towards Love itself. She discusses how bodily love is essentially preparing us for the reunion with the Divine:

> **Plato's Symposium 211-212**
>
> And so, when his prescribed devotion to boyish beauties has carried our candidate so far that the universal beauty dawns upon his inward sight, he is almost within reach of the final revelation. And this is the way, the only way, he must approach, or be led toward, the sanctuary of Love. Starting from individual beauties, the quest for the universal beauty must find him ever mounting the heavenly ladder, stepping from rung to rung--that is, from one to two, and from two to every lovely body, from bodily beauty to the beauty of institutions, from institutions to learning, and from learning in general to the special lore that pertains to nothing but the beautiful itself--until at last he comes to know what beauty is.

And if, my dear Socrates, Diotima went on, man's life is ever worth the living, it is when he has attained this vision of the very soul of beauty. And once you have seen it, you will never be seduced again by the charm of gold, of dress, of comely boys, or lads just ripening to manhood; you will care nothing for the beauties that used to take your breath away and kindle such a longing in you, and many others like you, Socrates, to be always at the side of the beloved and feasting your eyes upon him, so that you would be content, if it were possible, to deny yourself the grosser necessities of meat and drink, so long as you were with him.

But if it were given to man to gaze on beauty's very self – unsullied, unalloyed, and freed from the mortal taint that haunts the frailer loveliness of flesh and blood--if, I say, it were given to man to see the heavenly beauty face to face, would you call his, she asked me, an unenviable life, whose eyes had been opened to the vision, and who had gazed upon it in true contemplation until it had become his own forever?

And remember, she said, that it is when he looks upon beauty's visible presentment, and only then, that a man will be quickened with the true, and not the seeming, virtue--for it is virtue's self that quickens him, not virtue's semblance. And when he has brought forth and reared this perfect virtue, he shall be called the friend of god, and if ever it is given to man to put on immortality, it shall be given to him."

Knowledge

Matthew 17:20

"Truly I tell you, if you have faith as small as a mustard seed, you can say to this mountain, 'Move from here to there,' and it will move. **Nothing will be impossible for you.**"

With genuine faith, anything is possible. Do you believe this? Knowledge is helpful for facilitating faith; if you know you can do it, faith is fulfilled. Taking quantum physics into consideration, this makes sense. As demonstrated by the double-slit experiment, we as observers literally collapse probabilistic waveforms into concrete material substance. This means that our belief, or faith, has an effect on probability, and can manifest reality accordingly:

John 4:49-53

"The royal official went to him and begged him to come and heal his son, who was close to death… "Sir, come down before my child dies."

"Go," Jesus replied, "your son will live."

The man took Jesus at his word and departed. While he was still on the way, his servants met him with the news that his boy was living. When he inquired as to the time when his son got better, they said to him, "Yesterday, at one in the afternoon, the fever left him."

Then the father realized that this was the exact time at which Jesus had said to him, "Your son will live." So he and his whole household believed."

The moment that the father took Jesus's Word that his son would be ok, the son simultaneously was cured of his sickness. This demonstrates the dramatic, and instantaneous, effect of faith on manifestation. Quantum physics has demonstrated that entangled particles communicate with each other instantaneously, and are not limited to the speed of light. By putting our faith in God's will, we allow the transformation to occur. On the contrary, Jesus struggled to do miracles and heal those who strongly disbelieved:

Matthew 13:58

"And Jesus did not do many miracles there because of their lack of faith."

Even Jesus did less miracles among nonbelievers; this is how powerful faith is! Your beliefs have been molded from a very young age, and it is very difficult to change your core beliefs. If someone were to say "anything is possible", you would reflexively think, "That is not true". But, that is your belief. Because you believe this to be so, it has been perpetuated all your life. If you genuinely believe, without a glimmer of doubt, then it will be granted to you. Jesus tells us:

John 14:12

"Very truly I tell you, whoever believes in me will do the works I have been doing, **and they will do even greater things than these...**"

Why isn't this taught in church? Simple; the pastors do not even believe this. If they did, they would be performing miracles, healing the sick, etc. I struggle with this as well. Although I've had glimpses of pure, unadulterated faith that have manifested amazing things and healed minor ailments in people, I still struggle to perpetually hold genuine faith. This is partly why I am writing this book. By organizing all these ideas into a comprehensive statement about the authenticity of Christianity, I believe my faith will be facilitated. Best of all, just my mere belief that this will work, will make it work. Genuine belief is difficult, but Jesus told us how to facilitate our faith:

Matthew 17:20-21

"Truly I tell you, if you have faith as small as a mustard seed, you can say to this mountain, 'Move from here to there,' and it will move. Nothing will be impossible for you. However, this kind does not go out except by **prayer and fasting.**"

Praying, or meditating, allows us to analyze our wrong-doings, and thus purify our psyche from sin. This allows the God Mind to easily express itself without the veil of corruption. Fasting, which is to abstain from food, helps the body to become purified. Material things, including food, anchor us to the material realm, which we create. It is like getting trapped in our own creation. By fasting, you have faith that a higher sustenance will provide. This releases the heavy material anchors, and allows the expression of the God Mind. Jesus repeatedly states that he does nothing on his own unless it is through the Father (The God Mind).

John 4: 31-34

"In the meantime His disciples urged Him, saying, "Rabbi, eat.""

But He said to them, "I have food to eat of which you do not know."

Therefore the disciples said to one another, "Has anyone brought Him *anything* to eat?"

Jesus said to them, "My food is to do the will of Him who sent Me, and to finish His work."

Jesus' primary sustenance, as well as ours, is acting according with the Divine Plan. This is mentioned in Greek Philosophy as well:

Plato – Phaedo 83-84

"And this... is the reason why the true lovers of knowledge are temperate and brave; and not for the reason which the world gives... For not in that way does the soul of a philosopher reason; she will not ask philosophy to release her in order that when released she may deliver herself up again to the thraldom of pleasures and pains, doing a work only to be undone again, weaving instead of unweaving her Penelope's web. But she will make herself a calm of passion and follow Reason, and dwell in her, beholding the true and divine, which is not matter of opinion, **and thence derive nourishment**."

The pursuit of Truth literally nourished Jesus, and through the Father he did many great acts. This was possible because Jesus and the Father were (are) One. We too can join Them in God's Mind; it is just a matter of tuning our mindset accordingly, through psychological purification and release of extraneous attachments; this is the basis of all Jesus' teachings. Many have attained psychological purification, but are incapable of relieving extraneous attachments, i.e. material possessions. Spiritual possessions are psychological, and are "let in" by sinful behavior, which allows the aberrant spirit to reside in your psyche and thus distance your mind from God's. This is why repentance, which in Greek means "to change your mind", is so important. Relinquishing all evil thought allows the expression of the "I Am" in all of us. Yet, there is a subtle hindrance that few realize; material possessions.

Many think that they possess material things, when in actuality, those material things are possessing them. Observe how protective people are of their material possessions. These possessions are not taken lightly. By attaching yourself to material possessions, you are building barriers between you and the God Mind. This is why "false idols" are condemned. Many think it is harmless, but it is often the last roadblock that has prevented so many from entering the Kingdom in their lifetime:

Matthew 19:16-24

> Just then a man came up to Jesus and asked, "Teacher, what good thing must I do to get eternal life?"
>
> "Why do you ask me about what is good?" Jesus replied. "There is only One who is good. If you want to enter life, keep the commandments."
>
> "Which ones?" he inquired.
>
> Jesus replied, "'You shall not murder, you shall not commit adultery, you shall not steal, you shall not give false testimony, honor your father and mother,' and 'love your neighbor as yourself.'"
>
> "All these I have kept," the young man said. "What do I still lack?"
>
> Jesus answered, "**If you want to be perfect, go, sell your possessions and give to the poor, and you will have treasure in heaven. Then come, follow me.**"
>
> When the young man heard this, he went away sad, because he had great wealth.
>
> Then Jesus said to his disciples, "Truly I tell you, it is hard for someone who is rich to enter the kingdom of heaven. Again I tell you, it is easier for a camel to go through the eye of a needle than for someone who is rich to enter the kingdom of God."

This man who was seeking eternal life had a purified psyche, he kept all the commandments for spiritual purity, yet he was lacking because of his material possessions. He was not willing to give up his material possessions for a greater fulfillment, which Jesus claims is 100 times (100 symbolizes completeness) more than the splendors of our old "life". Jesus claims we can only be perfect once we dismiss our material possessions. Herein comes the virtue of faith. Faith that a higher sustenance will provide for us. Do not try this unless you genuinely believe it will work. Again, fasting helps facilitate faith because it releases the material anchors. Material possessions anchor us to this world, disallowing us to enter through the narrow gates to the Kingdom. If it is as Jesus said, and we will obtain the ability to "move mountains", then we will have no problem providing for ourselves, but taking this leap of faith is the difficult part that so few attempt, and even fewer have completed.

> **Matthew 7: 13-14**
>
> > "Enter through the narrow gate. For wide is the gate and broad is the road that leads to destruction, and many enter through it. But small is the gate and narrow the road that leads to life, and only a few find it."

The road that leads to life? Is this implying that we have not yet attained true life?

> **John 10:10**
>
> > "…I have come that they may have **life**, and have it to the **full**."

God is God of the Living. Surely He has the power to protect us from death, but so few find life, and end up dying. It is due to sin that we die (John 8:21, Romans 5:12), and while we sin, we remain a slave to sin. Liberating ourselves from sin allows freedom and the path to life.

> **John 14:6**
>
> > "I am the way and the truth and the life."

This Life He is referring to is transcendental. It is a completely unprecedented way of Living that makes our old life seem like a state of sleep-walking. Paul exemplifies this concept, and mentions it when discussing the New Covenant:

> **Romans 13:11**
>
> > "And do this, understanding the present time: The hour has already come for you to wake up from your slumber, because our salvation is nearer now than when we first believed."

We were dead in our sin, which means we were missing the point of life, but through finding Truth, we become alive. This awakening is the second birth that Jesus alludes to.

John 3:3-6

> Jesus replied, "Very truly I tell you, no one can see the kingdom of God unless they are born again."
>
> "How can someone be born when they are old?" Nicodemus asked. "Surely they cannot enter a second time into their mother's womb to be born!"
>
> Jesus answered, "Very truly I tell you, no one can enter the kingdom of God unless they are born of water and the Spirit. Flesh gives birth to flesh, but the Spirit gives birth to spirit."

This spiritual birth is the Son of Man. The Son of Man is thought to be strictly a reference to Jesus, but it is referring to the "new humanity". Jesus is like the vine to this new humanity, of which, the elect are to be branches of this vine, partaking in Life everlasting with Jesus as the metaphysical vine of the Universe.

John 15:1-17

> "I am the true vine, and my Father is the gardener. He cuts off every branch in me that bears no fruit, while every branch that does bear fruit he prunes so that it will be even more fruitful. You are already clean because of the word I have spoken to you. Remain in me, as I also remain in you. No branch can bear fruit by itself; it must remain in the vine. Neither can you bear fruit unless you remain in me.
>
> "I am the vine; you are the branches. If you remain in me and I in you, you will bear much fruit; apart from me you can do nothing. If you do not remain in me, you are like a branch that is thrown away and withers; such branches are picked up, thrown into the fire and burned. If you remain in me and my words remain in you, ask whatever you wish, and it will be done for you. This is to my Father's glory, that you bear much fruit, showing yourselves to be my disciples.
>
> "As the Father has loved me, so have I loved you. Now remain in my love. If you keep my commands, you will remain in my love, just as I have kept my Father's commands and remain in his love. I have told you this so that my joy may be in

you and that your joy may be complete. My command is this: Love each other as I have loved you. Greater love has no one than this: to lay down one's life for one's friends. You are my friends if you do what I command. I no longer call you servants, because a servant does not know his master's business. Instead, I have called you friends, for everything that I learned from my Father I have made known to you. You did not choose me, but I chose you and appointed you so that you might go and bear fruit—fruit that will last—and so that whatever you ask in my name the Father will give you. This is my command: Love each other."

The Son of Man, literally meaning the offspring of the human, is a spiritual birth. This "New humanity", is not physical, but spiritual:

John 3:13-15

"No one has ever gone into heaven except the one who came from heaven—the Son of Man. Just as Moses lifted up the snake in the wilderness, so the Son of Man must be lifted up, that everyone who believes may have eternal life in him."

Now we know the Son of Man is not strictly referring to Jesus, because Elijah and Enoch both ascended to heaven; it was the Son of Man, Elijah and Enoch's spiritual offspring, which rose into the heavens. That heavenly part of us has always resided in heaven, it is a matter of releasing the veil from our eyes which is caused by sin (material and spiritual possessions). The apocalypse does not mean doomsday, it means a "lifting of the veil". This is the great revelation, or revealing. This unveiling is the realization of our Spiritual nature, and thenceforth we explore the spiritual frontier:

Luke 9:57-60

As they were walking along the road, a man said to him, "I will follow you wherever you go."

Jesus replied, "Foxes have dens and birds have nests, but **the Son of Man has no place to lay his head.**"

He said to another man, "Follow me."

But he replied, "Lord, first let me go and bury my father."

Jesus said to him, "Let the dead bury their own dead, but you go and proclaim the kingdom of God."

This passage is very relevant to what has been discussed so far. A man asks to follow Jesus wherever he goes, yet Jesus says "The Son of Man has no place to lay his head". This indicates that the Son of Man is not physical, but rather, a spiritual entity. He furthers this conversation by asking someone to follow him, but the man asks to go bury his father. Jesus replies by saying "let the dead bury their own dead..." implying that the father, along with those who would bury him are essentially dead. They are not alive, but where Jesus is leading people is life. Dismiss the ways of the dead, and pursue the Kingdom of the Living.

When you have attained the wisdom and understanding of this new humanity, it is an obligation to act upon it. By doing this, you not only help others, but yourself as well. By teaching, you facilitate your own progress, and expedite the birth of the Son of Man and thus the reunion with the new humanity in God's Mind:

Matthew 10:23

> "When you are persecuted in one place, flee to another. Truly I tell you, you will not finish going through the towns of Israel before the **Son of Man** comes."

The apostles are told that the Son of Man will come before they finish teaching throughout Israel. This was demonstrated in the Acts of the Apostles; they healed the sick and were impervious to the violent leaders who sought to kill them for turning the people to Truth. The Church, or community, that they established was above the traditional law. This passage still applies to this day, although Israel can be thought of as nearby cities that are harboring the people of God – the harvest.

These transcendental teachings are not limited to Christianity. The idea that we are living in a sleep-walking daze, in a realm of decay, seeking liberation, is also the major theme in Greek Philosophy, and Hinduism. Plato, the great Greek philosopher, presents a parable. "The Allegory of The Cave", written around 380 BC, describes how we as humans are trapped in an illusion. The movie "The Matrix" is based off this allegory. This allegory describes prisoners, enslaved by their own ignorance, living in a cave in which their reality consists of shadows. They are ignorant to the fact that there is a deeper reality to these shadows. Upon practicing philosophy, they begin to discern between reality and illusion. As knowledge is obtained and practiced, they begin to see the light coming from outside and begin their ascent out of the cave; realizing that the shadows were only a vestige of the true reality. At first, the light, the true reality, outside the cave is overwhelming. The prisoner will be initially blinded by the light. But, eventually their eyes adjust and are able to approach the more real existence. Plato says we are like the prisoners and "...the journey upwards (is) the ascent of the soul into the intellectual world."

Jesus' teachings are essentially a how-to manual on escaping the cave and finding True Life outside the cave. In fact, Plato said that someone would come from outside the cave (from the light) to teach the cave-dwellers about the reality outside the cave; the cave-dwellers, in their ignorance, says Plato, would put this man to death! Written around 380 BC, This is a prophetic foretelling of the life of Christ. The ascent of the soul into the intellectual world is likened to the second birth of the Son of Man, which Paul, among others, exemplified. In Hinduism, this is called the escape from samsara, or Moksha. It is strongly advised that one should not stop seeking until they have found Life:

Matthew 7:7-8

> "Ask and it will be given to you; seek and you will find; knock and the door will be opened to you. For everyone who asks receives; the one who seeks finds; and to the one who knocks, the door will be opened."

Those seeking should not stop seeking until they have found. This is exemplified by Jesus being tempted in the wilderness. Upon forfeiting all material dependencies by fasting, he unveiled a whole new realm of possibility in which he was tempted with complete rulership of the world. Despite being offered endless material splendor, he refuses, because he knows that Spiritual fulfillment, Moksha, The Kingdom of Heaven, far surpasses, by 100x (implying True fulfillment), any splendor that the material world, the world of old, has to offer. Yet so many of us sell out for smaller degrees of material splendor. Many are complacent with barely surviving the material game. The devil raises the ante as you progress spiritually, because he knows that greater temptation is needed to get you to sell out to his falsehood.

The greatest feat the devil has ever performed is to convince the world that he does not exist. The bible explicitly states that the devil is a serpentine entity:

Revelation 12:9

> "The great dragon was hurled down—that ancient serpent called the devil, or Satan, who leads the whole world astray. He was hurled to the earth, and his angels with him."

This one passage, which may sound unbelievable at first, has much depth, and is a prophetic message that today holds many great truths. Steadfast your faith, because this will be a lot to swallow. The greatest feat the dragon has performed is to convince the world it does not exist; the world is convinced that the dragon is a mythological, imaginary entity.

What Were the Dinosaurs?

This section may be too much for someone who is strongly veiled by the world of old, the devil's realm of deception. Remember what quantum physics revealed to us through the double-slit experiment; it is the conscious observer that is integral to the working of the universe. Max Planck, nobel prize winning originator of quantum physics, reminds us that consciousness is the basis of reality. Creation through consciousness has already been discussed, so now we must dispel the lies we've been fed.

The word "dinosaur" was first used in 1842 by Sir Richard Owen to describe "fearfully great reptiles". All historical accounts before 1842 would not have used the word "dinosaur" to describe large reptilian creatures. Rather, large serpentine creatures prior to this date were called dragons, or were given a unique name:

Culture	Name for Dragon
China	Loong
Japan	Ryu
Philippines	Bakunawa
Indian	Naga
Khmer	Neak
Korean	Yong, Imoogi, Gyo
Vietnamese	Rong
Catalan	Drac
French	Dragon
Sardinian	Scultone
Scandinavian	Lindworm
English	Wyvern
Persian	Azhdaha
Slavic	Smok
Armenian	Vishap
Siberian	Yilbegan
Albanian	Kulshedra, Bolla, Dreq
Portugeese	Coca
Turkish	Evren
Lithuanian	Slibinas
Aztec	Quetzalcoatl
Incan	Pachamama
Mayan	Kukulkan
West African	Aido-Hwedo
Germany	Lindworm

Dragons are described in essentially all ancient cultures. In the Americas, Asia, Europe, Africa, and Australia, there are plenty of accounts that refer to large serpentine creatures; dragons. If this were a myth, this would mean that all these cultures coincidentally fabricated the same imaginary creature. Due to the geographic isolation of these cultures, separated by oceans and continents, we know this was not promulgated by diffusion of myth. Dragons are often described in a matter-of-fact manner without any implications of myth:

Herodotus – 5th Century B.C.

> "There is a place in Arabia, situated very near the city of Buto, to which I went, on hearing of some winged serpents; and when I arrived there, I saw bones and spines of serpents, in such quantities as it would be impossible to describe. The form of the serpent is like that of the water-snake; but he has wings without feathers, and as like as possible to the wings of a bat."

John de Trokelow – 14th Century A.D.

> "Close to the town of Bures, near Sudbury, there has lately appeared, the great hurt of the countryside, a dragon, vast in body, with a crested head, teeth like a saw, and a tail extending to an enormous length. Having slaughtered the shepherd of a flock, it devoured many sheep."

Marie Trevelyan – Folk-lore and Folk-stories of Wales

> "The legend connected with this stone pillar is, that it was raised in order to prevent the devastation which a winged serpent or dragon (a Wiber) was committing in the surrounding country. The stone was drapped with scarlet cloth, to allure and excite the creature to a furor, scarlet being a colour most intolerably hateful and provoking to it. It was studded with iron spikes, that the reptile might wound or kill itself by beating itself against it. Its destruction, is alleged, was effected by this artifice. It is said to have had two lurking places in the neighborhood, which are still called Nant-y-Wiber, one at Penygarnedd, the other near Bwlch Sychtyn, in the parish of Llansilin, and this post was in the direct line of its flight... In the ajoining parish of Llanarmon-Dyffryn-Ceiriog there is a place called Sarffle (the serpent's hole)"

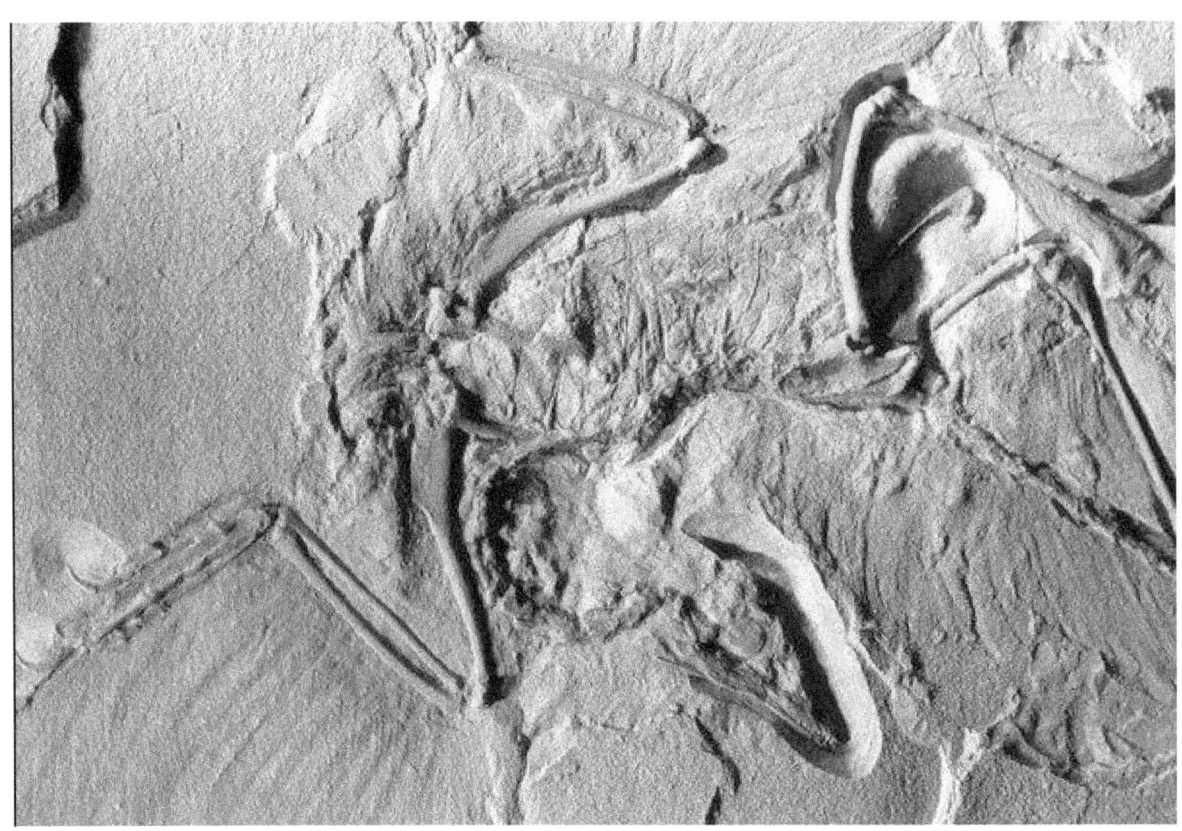

Marie Trevelyan – Folk-lore and Folk-stories of Wales

'The woods around Penllin Castle, Glamorgan, had the reputation of being frequented by winged serpents, and these were the terror of old and young alike. An aged inhabitant of Penllyne, who died a few years ago, said that in his boyhood the winged serpents were described as very beautiful. They were coiled when in repose, and "looked as if they were covered with jewels of all sorts. Some of them had crests sparkling with all the colours of the rainbow". When disturbed they glided swiftly, "sparkling all over," to their hiding places. When angry, they "flew over people's heads, with outspread wings, bright, and sometimes with eyes too, like the feathers in a peacock's tail". He said it was "no old story invented to frighten children", but a real fact. His father and uncle had killed some of them, for they were as bad as foxes for poultry. **The old man attributed the extinction of the winged serpents to the fact that they were "terrors in the farmyards and coverts"**

The extinction of these beasts is attributed to the havoc they reeked. Whether it be for pride or protection, dragons, all large serpentine creatures, were hunted and killed to the point of extinction.

Although the account above is deemed a folk-lore, its matter-of-fact wording insists that they were describing a real creature. It was some historians, without the understanding that dinosaurs (dragons) lived alongside humans, that deemed these accounts as mythological.

The Travels of Marco Polo, 1948, Book 2, Chapter XL, pg. 185-186

"Leaving the city of Yachi, and traveling ten days in a westerly direction, you reach the province of Karazan, which is also the name of the chief city....Here are seen huge serpents, ten paces in length (about 30 feet), and ten spans (about 8 feet) girt of the body. **At the fore part, near the head, they have two short legs, having three claws like those of a tiger**, with eyes larger than a forepenny loaf (pane da quattro denari) and very glaring."

The jaws are wide enough to swallow a man, the teeth are large and sharp, and their whole appearance is so formidable, that neither man, nor any kind of animal can approach them without terror. Others are met with of a smaller size, being eight, six, or 5 paces long; and the following method is used for taking them. In the day-time, by reason of great heat, they lurk in caverns, from whence, at night, they issue to seek their food, and whatever beast they meet with and can lay hold of, whether tiger, wolf, or any other, they devour;

"After which they drag themselves towards some lake, spring of water, or river, in order to drink. By their motion in this way along the shore, and their vast weight, they make a deep impression, as if a heavy beam had been drawn along the sands. Those whose employment is to hunt them observe the track by which they are most frequently accustomed to go, and fix into the ground several pieces of wood, armed with sharp iron spikes, which they cover with sand in such a manner as not to be perceptible.

When therefore the animals make their way towards the places they usually haunt, they are wounded by these instruments, and speedily killed. The crows, as soon as they perceive them to be dead, set up to scream; and this serves as a signal to the hunters, who advance the spot, and proceed to separate the skin from the flesh, taking care immediately to secure the gall, which is most highly esteemed in medicine.

In cases of the bite of a mad dog, a penny weight of it, dissolved in wine, is administered. It is also useful in accelerating parturition, when the labor pains of women have come on. A small quantity of it being applied to carbuncles, pustules, or other eruptions on the body, they are presently dispersed; and it is efficacious in many other complaints.

The flesh also of the animal is sold at a dear rate, being thought to have a higher flavor than other kinds of meat, and by all persons it is esteemed a delicacy."

The bolded part of the above excerpt indicates that these accounts are not referring to very long snakes, but rather, dragon-like creatures (Dinosaurs).

Sussex : St Leonard's Forest – 1614

"This serpent, or dragon as some call it, is reputed to be nine feete, or rather more, in length, and shaped almost in the form of an axletree of a cart: a quantitie of thickness in the middest, and somewhat smaller at both endes. The former part, which he shootes forth as a necke, is supposed to be an elle [3 ft 9 ins or 1 l4 cms] long; with a white ring, as it were, of scales about it. The scales along his back seem to be blackish, and so much as is discovered under his belie, appeareth to be red... it is likewise discovered to have large feete, but the eye may there be deceived, for some suppose that serpents have no feete ... [The dragon] rids away (as we call it) as fast as a man can run. His food [rabbits] is thought to be; for the most part, in a conie-warren, which he much frequents ...There are likewise upon either side of him discovered two great bunches so big as a large foote-ball, and (as some thinke) will in time grow to wings, but God, I hope, will (to defend the poor people in the neighbourhood) that he shall be destroyed before he grows capable of flight."

An old Assiniboine (Native American) story tells of a war party that:

> "...Traveled a long distance to unfamiliar lands and [saw] some large lizards. The warriors held a council and discussed what they knew about those strange creatures. They decided that those big lizards were bad medicine and should be left alone. However, one warrior who wanted more war honors said that he was not afraid of those animals and would kill one. He took his lance [a very old weapon used before horses] and charged one of the large lizard type animals and tried to kill it. But he had trouble sticking his lance in the creature's hide and during the battle he himself was killed and eaten."
> (Mayor, *Fossil Legends of the First Americans*, 2005, p. 294.)

The prolific 17th century writer Athanasius Kircher's recorded how the noble man, Christopher Schorerum, prefect of the entire territory, "wrote a true history summarizing there all, for by that way, he was able to confirm the truth of the things experienced, and indeed the things truly seen by the eye, written in his own words: 'On a warm night in 1619, while contemplating the serenity of the heavens, I saw a shining dragon of great size in front of Mt. Pilatus, coming from the opposite side of the lake [or 'hollow'], a cave that is named Flue [Hogarth-near Lucerne] moving rapidly in an agitated way, seen flying across; It was of a large size, with a long tail, a long neck, a reptile's head, and ferocious gaping jaws. As it flew it was like iron struck in a forge when pressed together that scatters sparks. At first I thought it was a meteor from what I saw. But after I diligently observed it alone, I understood it was indeed a dragon from the motion of the limbs of the entire body.' From the writings of a respected clergyman, in fact a dragon truely exists in nature it is amply established." (Kircher, Athanasius, *Mundus Subterraneus*, 1664, tr. by Hogarth, "Dragons," 1979, pp. 179-180.)

Notice that in many of the accounts above they are in disbelief when they see these large serpents; this means that by the 1600's there were very few of these large serpentine creatures remaining. Dragon was the generic term for a large reptile. Larger reptilian creatures with unique attributes were often given unique names. Various historical accounts describe creatures known today as dinosaurs. The following comes from Beowulf, an epic written somewhere near England between the 5th and 11th century AD:

> "Grendel's swift hard claws
> snatched at the first Geat
> He came to, ripped him apart, cut
> His body to bits with powerful jaws,
> Drank the blood from his veins and bolted
> Him down, hands and feet; death
> And Grendel's great teeth came together,
> Snapping life shut."

> "but their weapons
> Could not hurt him,
> the sharpest and hardest iron
> Could not scratch at Grendel's skin"

Does this creature sound familiar? Further clues:

> "The fiend reached for him with his claw, but he grasped it with set purpose, and threw his weight on Grendel's arm."

This monster had jaws that could devour humans whole, hard skin, it could bash through large doors, and had arms with claws. There is only one type of animal that fits this description: A Bipedal dinosaur such as the Tyrannosaurus Rex or the Allosaurus. This conclusion would be more widespread if more scholars were aware of human-dinosaur coexistence. "Grendel" (T-rex) also has a mother in the Beowulf saga, indicating there is nothing supernatural about this entity, but rather, this is a real biological creature. Also in Beowulf, a dragon is slain, coinciding with the aforementioned, matter-of-fact accounts of dragons.

The bible also mentions dinosaurs, but calls them dragons. The word dragon is used 25 times in the Old Testament. This is often omitted in more modern translations, because they presume that dragons are mythological! Surely enough, if you peruse a literal translation of the bible, it is clear that the authors were mentioning dragons. The best detailed account is given in the book of Job, which describes a dinosaur you may find familiar:

Job 40:15-23

> "Lo, I pray thee, Behemoth, that I made with thee: Grass as an ox he eateth.
>
> Lo, I pray thee, his power [is] in his loins, And his strength in the muscles of his belly.
>
> **He doth bend his tail as a cedar**, The sinews of his thighs are wrapped together,
>
> His bones [are] tubes of brass, His bones [are] as a bar of iron.
>
> He [is] a beginning of the ways of God, His Maker bringeth nigh his sword;
>
> For food do mountains bear for him, And all the beasts of the field play there.
>
> Under shades he lieth down, In a secret place of reed and mire.

Cover him do shades, [with] their shadow, Cover him do willows of the brook.

Lo, a flood oppresseth -- he doth not haste, He is confident though Jordan Doth come forth unto his mouth."

Behemoth has a tail likened to a cedar tree, hides underneath willow trees, limbs like forged metal, and is an herbivore. There is only one type of animal in history that fits this description: A Brachiosaurus-like creature. Notice how brachiosaurus is called a creature of God? This is because the brachiosaurus is a docile herbivore, emulating God's perfection. Grendel on the other hand, the tyrannosaurus rex described in Beowulf, is called "A Creation of Cain". This new understanding helps us solve the befuddling aspects of our history. The treacherous T-Rex was a thought-product of Cain, the cursed son of Eve. The Bible mentions another familiar dinosaur:

Job 41:1-34

"Can you pull in Leviathan with a fishhook
  or tie down its tongue with a rope?
Can you put a cord through its nose
  or pierce its jaw with a hook?
Will it keep begging you for mercy?
  Will it speak to you with gentle words?
Will it make an agreement with you
  for you to take it as your slave for life?
Can you make a pet of it like a bird
  or put it on a leash for the young women in your house?
Will traders barter for it?
  Will they divide it up among the merchants?
Can you fill its hide with harpoons-
  or its head with fishing spears?
If you lay a hand on it,
  you will remember the struggle and never do it again!
Any hope of subduing it is false;
  the mere sight of it is overpowering.
No one is fierce enough to rouse it.
  Who then is able to stand against me?

Who has a claim against me that I must pay?
    Everything under heaven belongs to me.
"I will not fail to speak of Leviathan's limbs,
    its strength and its graceful form.
Who can strip off its outer coat?
    Who can penetrate its double coat of armor[b]?
Who dares open the doors of its mouth,
    ringed about with fearsome teeth?
Its back has rows of shields
    tightly sealed together;
each is so close to the next
    that no air can pass between.
They are joined fast to one another;
    they cling together and cannot be parted.
Its snorting throws out flashes of light;
    its eyes are like the rays of dawn.
Flames stream from its mouth;
    sparks of fire shoot out.
Smoke pours from its nostrils
    as from a boiling pot over burning reeds.
Its breath sets coals ablaze,
    and flames dart from its mouth.
Strength resides in its neck;
    dismay goes before it.
The folds of its flesh are tightly joined;
    they are firm and immovable.
Its chest is hard as rock,
    hard as a lower millstone.
When it rises up, the mighty are terrified;
    they retreat before its thrashing.
The sword that reaches it has no effect,
    nor does the spear or the dart or the javelin.
Iron it treats like straw
    and bronze like rotten wood.
Arrows do not make it flee;
    slingstones are like chaff to it.

A club seems to it but a piece of straw;
   it laughs at the rattling of the lance.
Its undersides are jagged potsherds,
   leaving a trail in the mud like a threshing sledge.
It makes the depths churn like a boiling caldron
   and stirs up the sea like a pot of ointment.
It leaves a glistening wake behind it;
   one would think the deep had white hair.
Nothing on earth is its equal—
   a creature without fear.
It looks down on all that are haughty;
   it is king over all that are proud."

Leviathan is not as easy to identify as Grendel or Behemoth. We know its skin is hard, it drags its body in the mud, is likely aquatic in some regard (hence the fishhook), and attempting to capture it is a futile effort. It is the king of prideful animals, and is even claimed to be able to exhale fire. Isaiah disambiguates this mystery, and assures us this is a reference to a large serpentine creature, or dragon:

Isaiah 27:1
> "In that day lay a charge doth Jehovah, With his sword -- the sharp, and the great, and the strong, On leviathan -- a fleeing serpent, And on leviathan -- a crooked serpent, And He hath slain the **dragon** that [is] in the sea."

Fire-breathing sounds mythological, and it may be an embellishment, but it could have been possible. The bombardier beetle, an insect studied extensively in biology, is capable of spewing out a fiery expulsion from its abdomen. If dragons/dinosaurs were capable of exuding fire, it would not be reminiscent in their fossilized remains because a fire-generating organ, as seen in the bombardier beetle, would likely be made of soft tissue which decays too quickly to be fully observed thousands of years later. This brings up a good point; if dinosaurs/dragons are not as old as we think, shouldn't we be finding fossilized remains that have scraps of organic flesh, or soft tissue? Yes.

> "Soft fibrillar bone tissues were obtained from a supraorbital horn of *Triceratops horridus* collected at the Hell Creek Formation in Montana, USA. Soft material

was present in pre and post-decalcified bone... Filipodial extensions were delicate and showed no evidence of any permineralization or crystallization artifact and therefore were interpreted to be soft. This is the first report of sheets of soft tissues from *Triceratops* horn bearing layers of osteocytes, and extends the range and type of dinosaur specimens known to contain non-fossilized material in bone matrix."

(Armitage, MH; Anderson KL. (2013) Soft sheets of fibrillary bone from a fossil of the supraorbital horn of the dinosaur triceratops horridus. Acta Histochemica. 115(6), 603-608)

Soft tissue cannot last 10's or 100's of millions of years. Despite this fact, we continue to find soft tissue in dinosaur remains. This is not an anomaly. There have been plenty of other dinosaur bones that contain soft tissue. Dr. Mary Schweitzer found soft tissue in the fossilized remains of a Tyranosaurus rex (Grendel's not-so-distant cousin!), as well as a hadrosaur. Her work was verified by other scientists such as Phillip L. Manning:

"An extremely well-preserved dinosaur (*Cf. Edmontosaurus* sp.) found in the Hell Creek Formation (Upper Cretaceous, North Dakota) retains soft-tissue replacement structures and associated organic compounds. Mineral cements precipitated in the skin apparently follow original cell boundaries, partially preserving epidermis microstructure. Infrared and electron microprobe images of ossified tendon clearly show preserved mineral zonation, with silica and trapped carbon dioxide forming thin linings on Haversian canals within apatite. Furthermore, Fourier transform infrared spectroscopy (FTIR) of materials recovered from the skin and terminal ungual phalanx suggests the presence of compounds containing amide groups. Amino acid composition analyses of the mineralized skin envelope clearly differ from the surrounding matrix; however, intact proteins could not be obtained using protein mass spectrometry. The presence of endogenously derived organics from the skin was further demonstrated by pyrolysis gas chromatography mass spectrometry (Py-GCMS), indicating survival and presence of macromolecules that were in part aliphatic."

[Manning et al. (2009) Mineralized soft-tissue structure and chemistry in a mummified hadrosaur from the Hell Creek Formation, North Dakota (USA). Proc Biol Sci. 3429-3437.]

Furthermore, in "DNA sequence from Cretaceous period bone fragments" published in Science Magazine, the researchers found DNA sequences in "80-million-year-old bone fragments". These sequences were long enough to elucidate coding for mitochondrial cytochrome b. The old dogma of a billion year old earth has blinded scientists to the truth; these dinosaur remains are not millions of years old. The researchers back-track and claim "small fragments of DNA may survive in bone for millions of years", while refusing to consider the more logical answer that dinosaurs are only thousands of years old. Due to this common misconception, these researchers do not even carbon date these findings because carbon-dating does not work past 100,000 years. Their prejudice prevents them from discerning the truth of these fossils. This prejudice is explained by John Michael Fischer, who discusses the bias that was involved when carbon-dating proved dinosaurs are thousands of years old. The following is from www.newgeology.com:

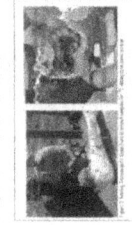

Carbon-dating, albeit unreliable, indicates these specimens are less than 40,000 years old. This clearly indicates that life is not hundreds of millions of years old. The fact that dinosaur remains contain soft tissue lets us know that dinosaurs were present thousands of years ago. Soft tissue decays quickly. Here is a time lapse picture of a decaying pig:

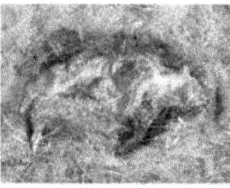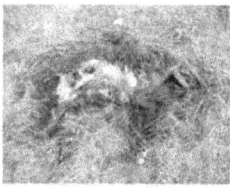

The fact that Mary Schweitzer found remnants of blood vessels in the "65 million year old" T-Rex fossil speaks for its self. The T-Rex she found was living thousands of years ago, not millions. I could understand skepticism if it were rare to find soft tissue in dinosaur fossils, but now that researchers know where to look, it seems to be the norm. Once it is more acceptable to consider that the old-earth dogma may be wrong, then we will make true progress.

Mark Armitage, who found soft tissue in the triceratops remains, was subsequently fired by California State University after publishing his research. You cannot publish results evidencing a young-earth, while supporting such a conclusion, and remain in the scientific community.

It is difficult discerning historical documents that may or may not be describing dinosaurs. There is also the potential that they were coincidentally mythologizing creatures that were similar to dinosaurs. Although photography did not exist back then, we do have artistic representations that strongly insist that various cultures were in direct contact with dinosaurs/dragons.

In Cambodia, the Ta Prohm temple is ornamented with extravagant carvings of various living animals. Amongst these depictions of living creatures is the carving above. This seems to be a detailed carving of a stegosaurus-like creature; as indicated by the plates along its back.

The pictures to the right are Ancient Chinese ornaments. These Protoceratops look-alikes are estimated at 4000 years olds. The head crest seen on these ornaments is reminiscent of the protoceratop's head.

The pictures to the left is a Sauroloophus figurine from the Shang Dynasty estimated between the 18th and 12th century BC.

Next there is some familiar pictures of our friend Behemoth. The brachiosaurus, and dinosaurs like it, would surely have been depicted by various cultures due to its immense size. Surely enough, there are plenty of pictorial representations of it throughout history. Below is a Mesopotamian cylinder seal, which is currently housed at the Louvre:

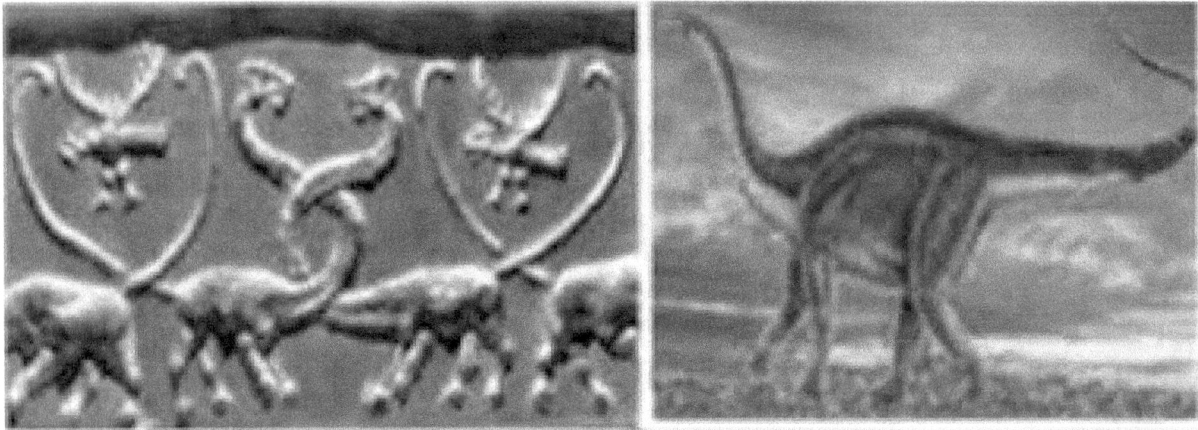

The following are Egyptian palettes, which are similar to the above Mesopotamian piece:

67

If you look close you can see serrations in the neck of these brachiosaurus-like creatures. Surely such accentuated neck muscles would have been necessary for supporting such a long neck. There is another peculiar commonality, which at first glance looks like it may be an ear. But if we examine the skull of the brachiosaurus we realize it has a bulbous cranial apparatus at the top of its skull:

This cranial protuberance is evident in all these brachiosaurus depictions. Look closely at the top of their heads, what may look like an ear at first, may actually be a representation of this cranial anomaly. Brachiosaurus depictions are not limited to the middle-east region, in fact, there are many ancient paintings that clearly indicate that the artist was observing a brachiosaurus. Below is a picture drawn by the Anasazi North Americans in modern day Utah:

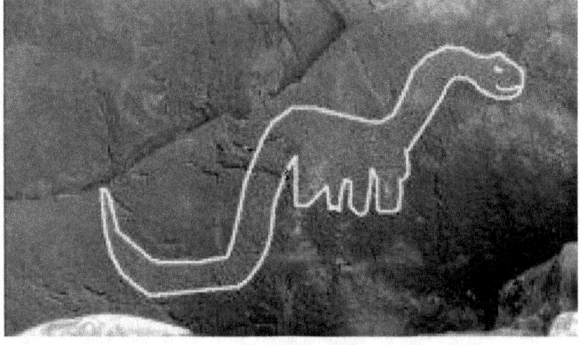

Utah

And below is a picture from the Amazon:

These magnificent dinosaurs were also depicted as far as northern England, near the border of Scotland. The following is a photo of the encryptions on the tomb of Bishop Bell, who was buried in 1496.

Just like the Cambodians depicted the stegosaurus at the Ta Prohm Temple, a pre-Greek civilization residing in Southern Italy were crafting terracotta statues resembling a similar dinosaur:

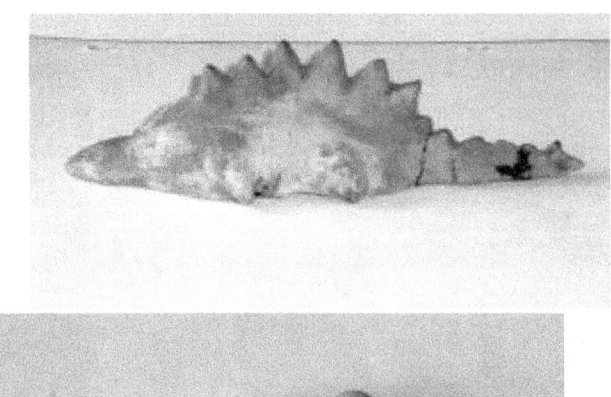

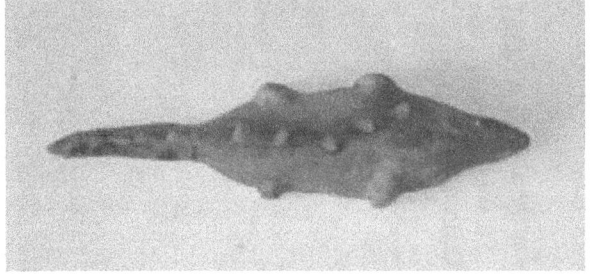

Before we continue, sit back and organize this immense body of evidence. Remember, "dinosaur" was not a word until around 1850, any large serpentine creature described prior to this date, and shortly after this date, would have been called a dragon, or given a specific name such as Grendel, Behemoth, or Leviathan. These artistic representations are further proof that our ancestors walked with dinosaurs.

"The Nile Mosaic of Palestrina", located in southern Rome, depicts scenes from Africa, including Egypt and Ethiopia. The mosaic contains a group of dark-skinned hunters chasing a dinosaur-like creature. Next to this creature is the word "KROKODILOPARDALIS", which means crocodile-leopard; indicating that his creature was an agile reptilian creature.

The Chinese have extensive documentation of the dragon, or dinosaur, but unfortunately modern scholars have incorrectly deemed it mythology. The following is from 1500 BC:

This agile-looking dragon is reminiscent of the Palestrina Mosaic that depicted the "Crocodile-leopard". With all this evidence, literary, artistic, and scientific, it is undoubtable that humans lived with living dinosaurs.

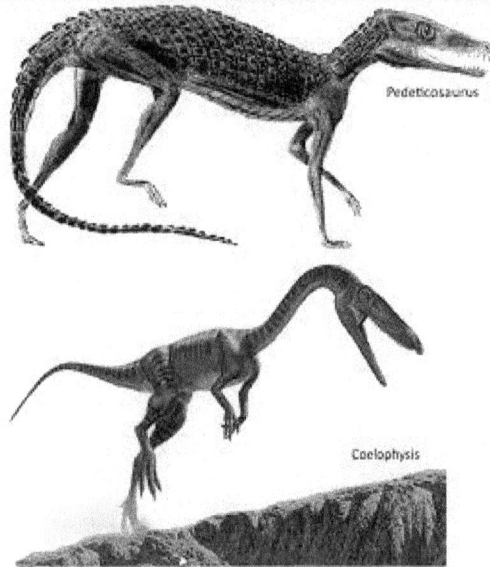

Below is an altar cloth from a chapel in Barcelona. This monster is reminiscent of the nothosaurus, which is an amphibious dinosaur; meaning it roamed on land and water. Barcelona is along the coast of modern day Spain, indicating that these people would likely have correlated dragons (large reptilian creatures) with nothosaurs. This is indicated in their art. (Nothosaur picture thanks to M&G Therin-Weise)

Maps often depict dragons as well. Many old maps contain the phrase "hic sunt dracones" which means, "here be dragons". Again, because historians think dragons are mythological, they claim "here be dragons" is an idiom for saying "here be unknown things". From "Diccionari Tehuelche", the historian Rodolfo Casamiquela displays a 16th century map of what is now known as Argentina/Brazil:

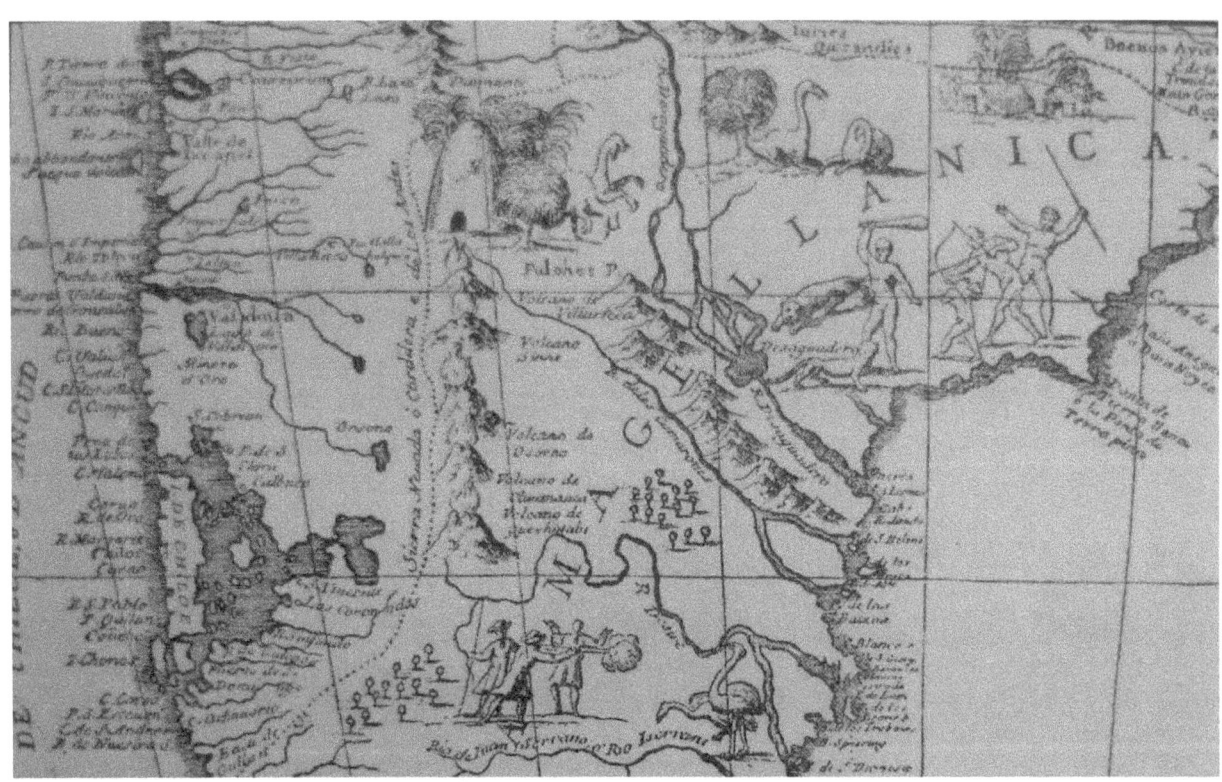

In the Colorado Rockies, the Granby Idol was unearthed by WL Chalmers near Grand Lake. While renovating his homestead, he found a 66 pound stone, along with various ancient tools, several feet below the surface. The stone was made of a very hard green substance. Jean Allard Jeancon, archaeologist and curator of the Colorado Historical and Natural History Society, claimed in "Le Grand Reporter", in 1923, that "If this stone can be proven genuine, it is the biggest find in all anthropological research and antedate anything on the American continent and is going to establish the remote antiquity of man. I have never seen such remarkable outline of dinosaurs and mastodons!" Unbeknownst to Professor Jeancon, it was not man's extended history that was in question, but rather, a more recent date for dinosaurs. Unfortunately, this stone was "lost" by the museum. Luckily, someone took a picture before the artifact was lost:

A painting salvaged from Pompeii, the southern Italian town notoriously destroyed by volcanic eruption, depicts dinosaur-like creatures (thanks to www.marine-antique.net):

Just like Grendel was deemed a mythological creature from the Epic of Beowulf, there is another familiar dinosaur that has been mythologized along the ages. The Tarasque is a strange 6-legged creature with familiar plating on its backside. According to legend, the Tarasque terrorized a medieval town until finally being slain by the villagers. This original creature that was killed by the villages has been exaggerated ever since, and was given an extra pair of legs and the obvious fabrication of a human face:

When the two are seen side by side, it is quite obvious that the Tarasque was an embellishment of the ankylosaur.

Tarasque

Ankylosaurid

Tarasque Statue

Ankylosaurid Statue

Above is Sirrush, which means "splendor serpent", painted on the Ishtar gate of Babylon. It is clearly a serpentine creature with scales and claws. Also on the gate are lions and other commonly known animals. In "Bel and the Dragon", Nebuchadnezzar planned to sacrifice the prophet Daniel to the dragon. They wanted to test Daniel's invisible God against their living god. Daniel prevailed by poisoning the beast, the Babylonian's "living god".

If all this is true, then the fossil record should match as well. It does. Trilobites are tiny creatures thought to be hundreds of millions of years old. Disputing this baseless claim is the Meister print, which shows a sandal print that stepped on top of a trilobite.

This track, "The Delk Print", is from Glen Rose, Texas nearby the Paluxy River. This finding is amazing. It was verified by X-ray and CT scanning procedures which proved this was not a fraudulent carving, but was an actual print. This was shown by densification of the limestone right underneath the prints, which demonstrated that these were caused by real footprints. This is the holy grail for human and dinosaur cohabitation.

Dr Carl Baugh

"The compression lines, the density features, do show, and there is no way to fake that," he said. "It is possible to carve a track in limestone. But there is no way to compress the material in the rock under the track. That is absolutely impossible. That's why the CAT scans are so important."

This evidence has left the skeptics speechless. One refute is that the big toe depression should not be that much deeper than the rest of the toes. But, this is nonsense. Of course the big toe would bear the greatest load from the distribution of weight during a human step. Despite the CT scan proving that the dinosaur track is also genuine, skeptics say it is too perfect. It is likely that the dinosaur was walking when it made its print, whereas the human was jogging or running. Because this material is limestone, tampering is easily spotted. If this were fake it would have been shown in the CT scans. There were no signs of tampering.

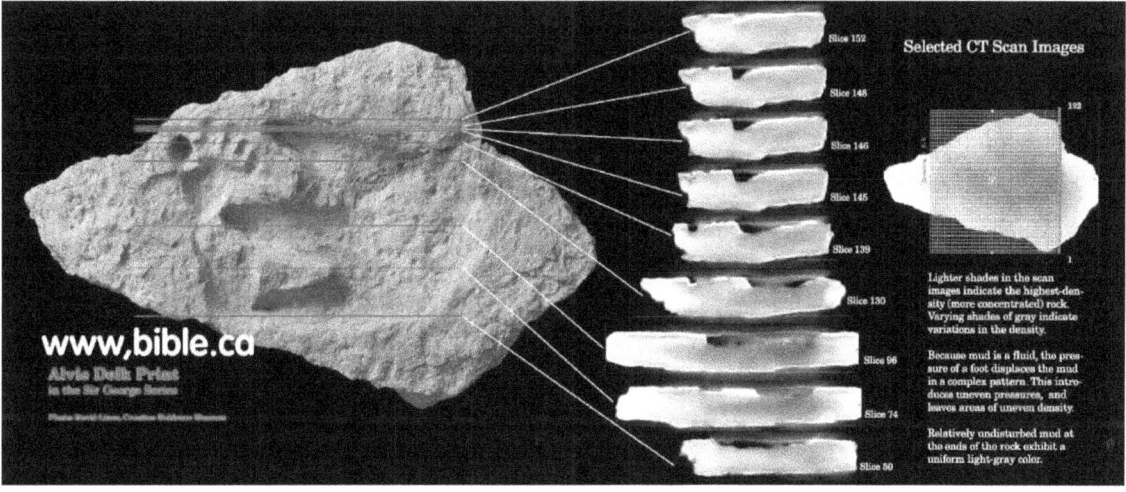

Cultures all over the earth have written descriptions and artistic depictions of dinosaurs. The quantity of these accounts proves these are not mere coincidences. Scientists are finding DNA, blood cells, and other organic material in dinosaur remnants; demonstrating these organisms did not die millions of years ago. Carbon dating disproves the million year old theory. The decay process is too fast for this remaining organic tissue to survive for millions of years, especially when no extraordinary form of preservation is exhibited. We also find dinosaur tracks in the same geologic strata as human remains. The information presented in this chapter is only the tip of the iceberg. There are many other findings that prove that dinosaurs are not millions of years old. I strongly insist the seekers of the truth do not act according to bias, but adhere to facts. The truth will be revealed, it is just a matter of uncovering it. The more people know about all this evidence, the sooner mainstream science will be able to assimilate these ideas and thoroughly test them. Then the absolute truth will be known.

How to Descend into the 2nd Dimension

What if the most prolific false idol ever to attract humankind was on earth right now? What if this idol was also the culmination of the false light of Lucifer? Would you be able to guess what it is? Lucifer, the false light, who comes resembling an angel of light, has hastened his spirit into the advancement of electricity which gave rise to the most distracting idol of all time: the cell phone.

With that being said, it must be admitted that the technological boom has brought humanity to an unprecedented stage of advancement. This advancement is a double-edged sword. It presents us with an endless access to knowledge, but it has enthralled our spirits with its superfluous luxury and entertainment. This is most evident with the cell phone. It is ever-increasing in ability, and the user is becoming more and more captivated.

It appears as though the zombie apocalypse has already started. Despite the endless access to knowledge presented on the internet, there is an apparent dislodgement from the present moment of reality that coincides with habitual cell phone use. This problem is somewhat reminiscent of Plato's Cave Allegory, in which 2-dimensional images distract people from the true reality (the light) residing outside the cave. But, an even more accurate prophecy is present in the book of Revelation. The notorious mark of the beast.

Revelation 13:15

> "and there was given to it to give a spirit to the **image** of the beast, that also the **image of the beast may speak**..."

A speaking image. Take a moment to reflect on this. This is a reference to all 2D speaking images; TV's, cell phones, laptops, etc. All made possible by electricity, the false light of Lucifer. Think about it, we don't put our faith in God, we put our faith in technology.

Psalm 31:6

"I hate those who cling to worthless idols; as for me, I trust in the LORD."

If the false light, electricity, were to suddenly stop working, a panic would ensue because so many are completely dependent upon it. What you do about this fact is up to you, but it is suggested that you start reintroducing yourself to nature, and renouncing your faithful reliance on technology. Sustainable living is going to help you and the world as a whole.

As technology is advancing, we are seeing all of these different 2D image devices integrate with one another; TV programming has come to the phone, and the world wide web is now accessible through all of these devices. The world wide web was also predicted in revelation:

Revelation 13:8

"Here is the wisdom! He who is having the understanding, let him count the number of the beast, for the number of a man it is, and its number [is] **666**."

The notorious 666. But, what does it mean? The Jewish alphabet is intimately linked to a numerical system. It is commonly known that all letters are represented by numerical values. This is called Gematria:

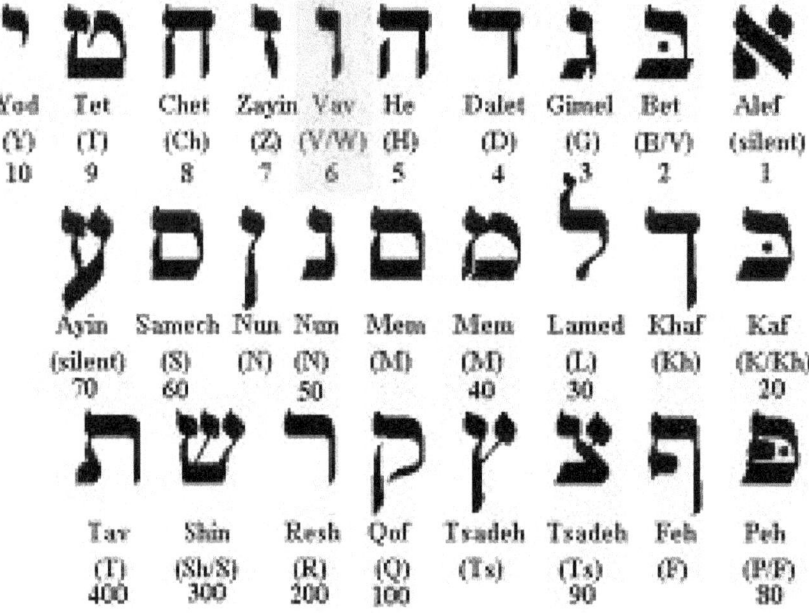

By arithmetic manipulation, 666 has been proposed to mean Nero Caesar. But, without any manipulation whatsoever, taking 666 at face value, we can see the true revelatory vision of John. The number 6 is attributed to the letter W. 666 can be synonymous with WWW: the world wide web. This is the number of the beast, or, in other words, the medium by which the beast can operate. Through its access to the internet, our 2-Dimensional cell phone images have immense possibility. The cell phone is either used in our hands, or placed to our heads when using it, and mostly all people have one whether they are rich or poor:

Revelation 13:16

> "And it maketh all, the small, and the great, and the rich, and the poor, and the freemen, and the servants, that it may give to them a mark upon their right hand or upon their foreheads,"

Nowhere does it say that this is a permanent mark. This is something temporary, like an idol that we can change in a whim. Also, from reading other passages that use the word "forehead", we can assume that this is also inferring that this mark will enthrall our thoughts, or "be in mind":

Revelation 14:1

> "Then I looked, and there before me was the Lamb, standing on Mount Zion, and with him 144,000 who had his name and his Father's name written on their **foreheads**."

This makes it clear that the phrase 'on their foreheads' is synonymous with "on your mind". It is also literally placed on our heads to be used. As we all know, our cellphones are constantly on our minds. We are compulsively checking our cell phones for unread message. We look at them to avert silence or awkward circumstances. It is distancing us from genuine human interaction. Not only that, but it can divert our mindset away from the God Mind. This is the ominous aspect to the cell phone. Surely, the endless access to information presented on the world wide web is a benefit for obtaining knowledge. This has allowed anyone to learn anything they could want. Despite this, True Knowledge was always present in the Bible, so this endless access to information is superfluous because all the knowledge we need for our soul's ascent is in the Bible. Also, this does not mean that anyone who used a cell phone is condemned, but rather, it is important that you are aware of the addictive aspect of the image of the beast, and everyone should be encouraged to ween off of relying on it. Remove your faith from the beast, and return to God.

By being cognizant of this, you can use the world wide web for learning, rather than distraction. For example, this book you are reading would have taken decades to write without the help of the internet.

When addressing the ascent of the soul into the light, which Einstein proved was the 4th dimension ("Evolution of Physics": Einstein), we can see how this 2-dimensional reality, or the image of our cell phone, would be the ultimate detractor for those seeking a Higher Reality. We are purposed to enter extra-dimensional reality, transcendent of the limitations of time in pure light. But, enthrallment with our smart-screens could prevent such an ascent into the light if the individual is not cognizant of its addictive aspect.

Revelation 22:5

"There will be no more night. They will not need the light of a lamp or the light of the sun, for the Lord God will give them light. And they will reign for ever and ever."

1 Thessalonians 5:5

"Ye are all the children of light, and the children of the day: we are not of the night, nor of darkness."

Ephesians 5:8

"For ye were sometimes darkness, but now *are ye* light in the Lord: walk as children of light"

Matthew 5:14

"Ye are the light of the world. A city that is set on an hill cannot be hid."

Jesus is the scaffold of this light. His teachings are there for us to learn how to integrate with the light:

John 8:12

"Again, therefore, Jesus spake to them, saying, `I am the light of the world; he who is following me shall not walk in the darkness, but he shall have the **light of the life**.'"

This is the meaning of "enlightenment", and also the following passage:

John 1:4-9

"In him was life, and the life was the light of men, and the light in the darkness did shine, and the darkness did not perceive it. There came a man -- having been sent from God -- whose name [is] John, this one came for testimony, that he might testify about the Light, that all might believe through him; that one was not the Light, but -- that he might testify about the Light. He was the true Light, which doth enlighten every man, coming to the world"

This sort of enlightenment involves us reducing our material weight. The cell phone is the ultimate culmination of material distraction, if used incorrectly. Those who praise this image, without the God Mind first and foremost in thought, will face the consequence of idolatry. This isn't as though God will send down lightning bolts to hurt them, but rather, the consequences of cell phone addiction are self-inflicted, and result in social awkwardness, reduced attention span, various ailments of the eye, etc. This distracts us and separates us from the God Mind. Revelation discusses what sounds like some sort of radiation sickness resulting from the beast:

Revelation 16:2

> "...and the first did go away, and did pour out his vial upon the land, and there came a sore -- bad and grievous -- to men, those having the mark of the beast, and those bowing to his image."

The world wide web has been an increasingly popular place to purchase items. We are also seeing an integration of credit cards into our cell phones, using the world wide web as its medium. This is where we see programs such as "Apple Pay", "Virtual Wallet", etc. These phone programs will soon take over the credit card market, and it would be economically viable for cell phone companies to monopolize this advantage they have. Cell phone companies will take over the role of credit cards, and integrate them into their software; this would significantly increase their profits, and it is already being executed. This integration has already begun. This was also predicted in Revelation:

Revelation 13:17

> "...and that no one may be able to buy, or to sell, except he who is having the mark, or the name of the beast, or the number of his name."

Remember, the number of its name is WWW. This passage is eluding to the ever-approaching ubiquity of not only the internet market, but also the imminent integration of credit card payment into our cell phones. I would presume this world will wrap up around the time when you can only pay with your cell phone or the internet and physical cash is no longer used. My best guess would be that this will occur in about 10 years, when cash may be as inconvenient, and undesirable as coin change is today in 2016. Why carry cash or credit cards when it could all be on your phone? This is where the phone companies are headed. The only reason this has not already come to pass is that the credit card companies are holding on for dear life. Increased security, and decreased fraudulent charges will be promulgated with cell phone integration, indicating this will be the future of monetary transactions.

The cell phone is by far the best candidate for the mark of the beast. Take into consideration the confusion that John, the supposed author of Revelation, must have been experiencing when he saw the cell phone in his great vision. He did a fine job describing it. Since the Word is our foundation, He was able to tap into the prophetic number 666. Since numbers are related to letters, John was essentially tapping into the coding of the universe, and was able to get a glimpse of what was to come when the final revelation would occur. Since everyone surfing the internet is expressing www, it is one of the most commonly expressed sequence of letters (numbers) in the history of humanity, and therefore John was able to pick up on this due to his intimate connection with God Mind, which is transcendent of time, the Alpha-Omega.

Because the word works through symbolism, the Apple logo is indicative of eating the forbidden fruit:

Heavenly Arithmetic: The Human Body

Since the human is an intelligent creation, there are many mathematical patterns present within the body. Phi (Φ) and pi (π), are irrational number, meaning that their decimal places go on infinitely without repeating any sequence of numbers. Therefore, an infinitude of information is programmed into these numbers. These two numbers are integral to nature, and are more common than you may think.

The phi ratio, approximately 1.618… , also known as the "divine proportion" or the "golden ratio" is all over the human body. The key proportions of your body resemble the phi ratio. Antony Davis of the Indian Statistical Institute, and Rudolf Altevogt of the Zoologisches Institut der Universitat studied the phi ratio in the body and its consistency among a population. They found that from the foot to the belly button, and 0then from the belly button to the top of the head consistently manifests the phi ratio. This is shown by dividing E by D (E/D) in the following picture:

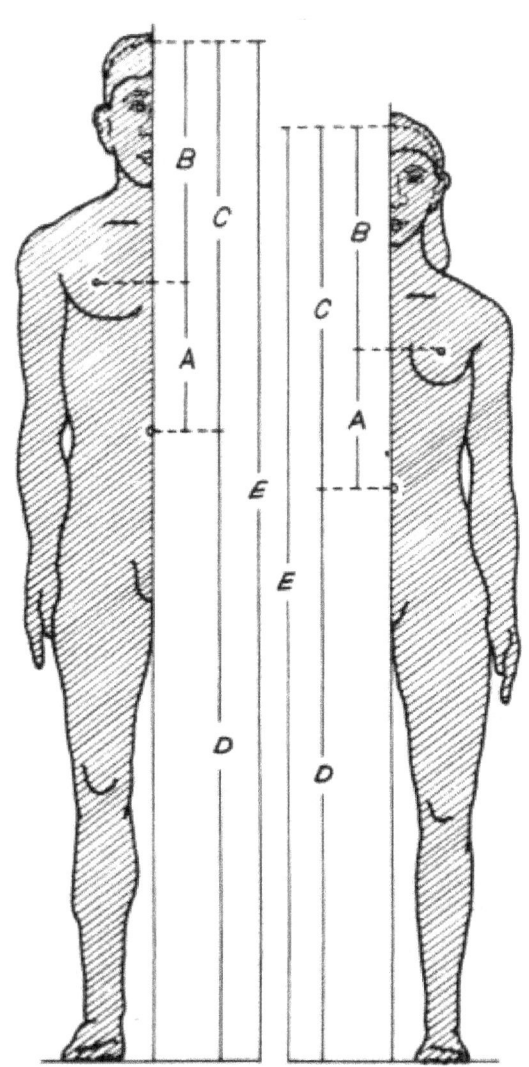

The average of this ratio among over 200 German students was 1.618, and was 1.615 among over 200 native Calcutta residents. D/C also approximates to phi. C/B also approximates to phi, this is the distance of the head to the navel divided by the head to the nipple. It appears as though beauty may be mathematical and manifests as the phi ratio. Phi is the proportion to which our body was designed.

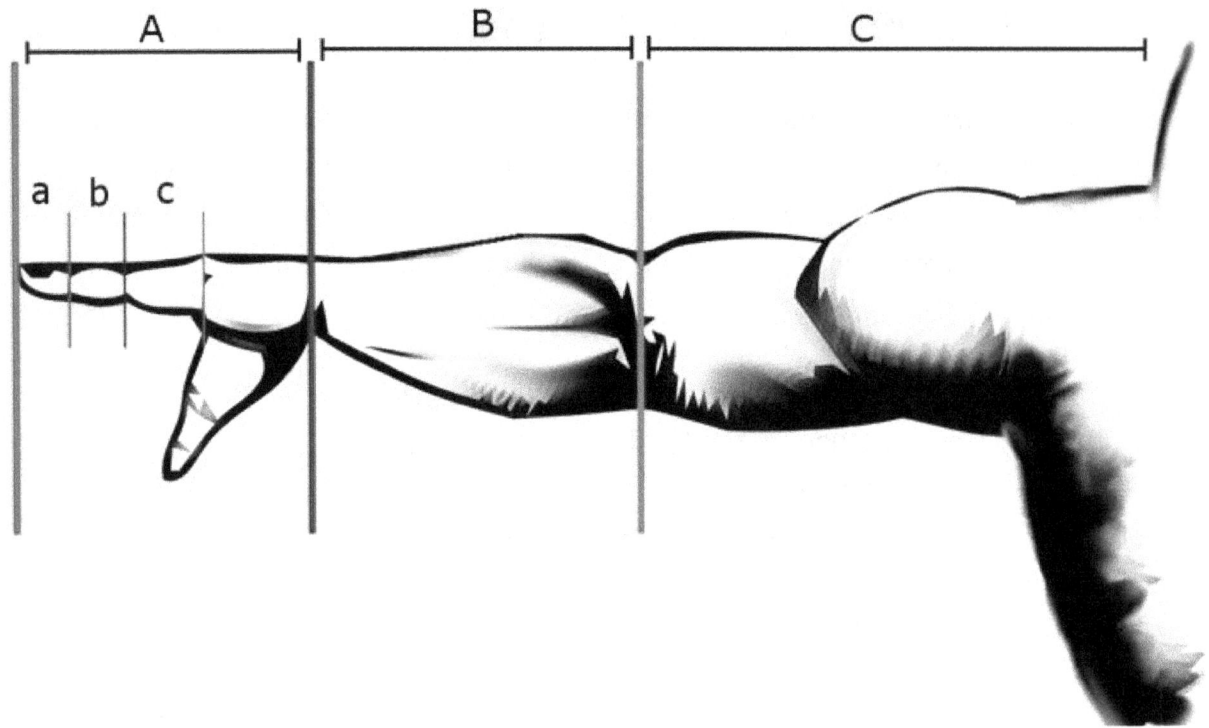

    The bones in your fingers resemble the phi ratio. In the arm diagram, b/a and c/b create the phi ratio. The arm follows the same pattern, B/A and C/B create the phi ratio. In other words, your forearm length divided by your hand length is phi. The bones of your finger also are proportioned according to phi.

    The phi ratio is also present in the face. The ratio of the distance from your chin to the middle of your eyes, and your chin to the middle of your lips is phi. The ratio from your eyes to your chin, over the distance from your eyes to your hairline is also phi:

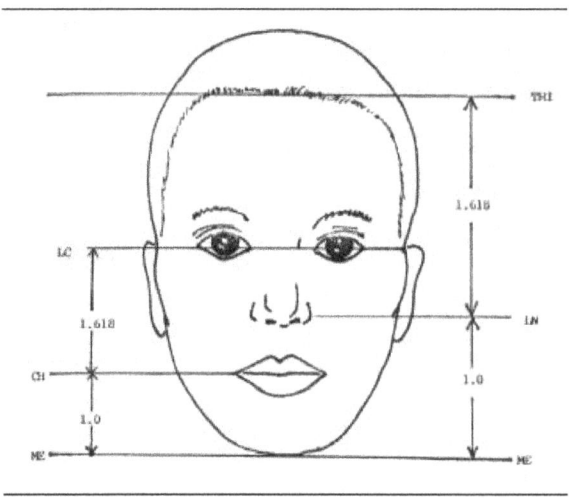

This ratio is also present in the horizontal dimensions of the face. The width of the nose (ends of nostrils), the width of the lips (corner to corner), the outer distance of the eyes (lateral end to lateral end), and the width of the forehead are all in phi proportions.

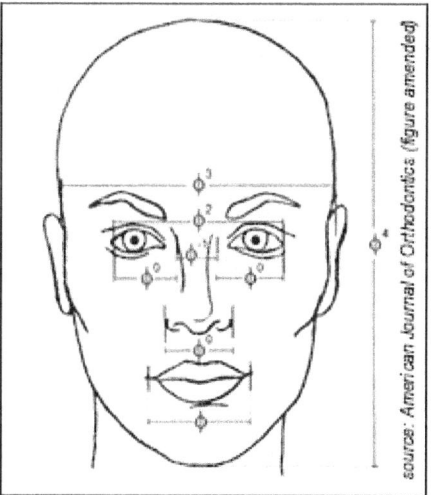

The phi ratio is commonly presented as a spiral. This is done by multiplying the side of a square by phi, and then using that length to make a rectangle with the square inside:

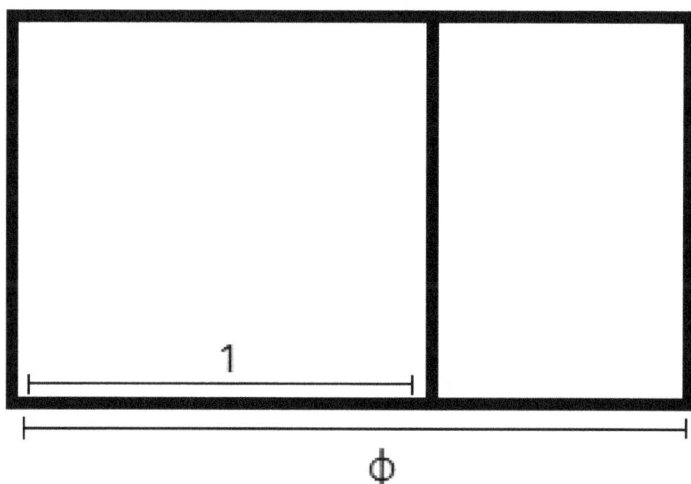

You can continue this pattern and it will create the phi spiral, most commonly noticed in the human ear:

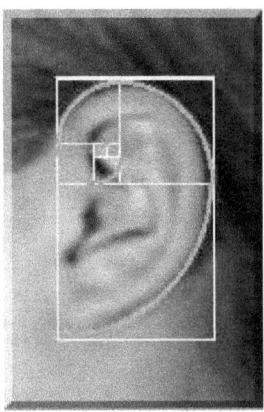

This spiral is also common inside of our body as well. Most notable is the cochlea, which is responsible for processing incoming sound waves.

Branching, as seen in arteries, veins, and trees approximately follows the phi ratio. It is also evident in the pinecone, which resembles the pineal gland. Thus, the pineal gland is indicative of the fractal nature of our consciousness, it is a pattern that goes on infinitely into the Mind of God. There are many, many other examples of the presence of phi, and I encourage anyone to continue this research.

Pi, approximately 3.14..., is another number, like phi, present throughout creation. Any spherical object, or object approximating a sphere, naturally has pi present within its coding. This is because pi is calculated when you divide the circumference of a circle by its diameter. Common spherical objects include planets, suns, eyeballs, cells, jellyfish, etc. These exemplify the fact that intelligent design is the foundation of our universe; pi and phi are irrational numbers, numbers which are inconceivable by our fallen intellect. Therefore, this Intelligence that created us, also created the outside world as well (Matthew 23: 25-26). If we are currently incapable of understanding these concepts, then surely we are still alienated from the creator, but, through knowledge, we come to Know.

Many put limitations on the human body. But, it is capable of "miraculous" feats. A common medical miracle is cardiac angiogenesis in response to heart attacks. A heart attack occurs due to blockage in the arteries surrounding the heart, thus starving the heart muscles of oxygen. It is common that arteries will naturally develop to bypass the blocked arteries, and re-establishing a complete circuit to the heart. We should relinquish the self-imposed limitations we put on our body. This allows us to realize its true potential.

Many think they are doomed to their genetics. This is not the case. Epigenetics is the field of study that involves the dynamic nature of the expression of your genetic code. In other words, the study of gene malleability. This field has proven that behavior and mindset have a magnificent impact on the workings of the body. One study, "Rapid changes in histone deacetylases and inflammatory gene expression in expert meditators", demonstrated that mental mechanisms, i.e. changing one's thoughts, or 'Repentance', was able to drastically change the expression of a certain inflammatory gene. Normally, inflammation is the body's healing mechanism. Inflammation can raise to aberrant levels and actually be a disease correlate, as seen in Alzheimer's, gout, psoriasis, etc, rather than a bodily benefactor. This experiment, among many others, demonstrated the profound effect of mindset on the expression of inflammatory genes. Those who prayed or meditated in the study were able to decrease the excessive inflammation that was manifesting as disease. We can safely assume that mostly all bodily mechanisms have epigenetic malleability, and thus are constantly being influenced by our mindset and behavior.

The effect of our mindset, or belief, on various medical outcomes has been called the placebo effect. The placebo effect shows that patients who believe they are receiving a beneficial treatment will receive a noticeable physiological benefit, despite being fed nothing but a fake pill. The placebo effect is ubiquitous in studies involving a human patient, and is so strong that all studies are encouraged to involve a placebo group to account for the tremendous impact that belief has on patient outcome. This is a friendly reminder to the idea of healing through faith. In mostly all Jesus' healings, the patient's faith is the facilitator of the cure:

Matthew 9:22

> Jesus turned and saw her. "Take heart, daughter," he said, "your **faith** has healed you." And the woman was healed at that moment.

Mark 2:5, 11-12

> When Jesus saw their **faith**, he said to the paralyzed man, "Son, your sins are forgiven" ..."I tell you, get up, take your mat and go home." He got up, took his mat and walked out in full view of them all...

Mark 10:52

> "Go," said Jesus, "your **faith** has healed you." Immediately he received his sight and followed Jesus along the road.

Faithlessness disempowers such healing ability: "…And (Jesus) did not do many miracles there because of their lack of faith" (Matthew 13:58). We have free will, and through choosing sin, we die due to our ontological perversion. This is the becoming process in which we are introduced to Being – the I Am Presence with God. Sin is unbecoming, straying us from this integration process. Through faith sins are forgiven.

Luke 5:20

"When Jesus saw their faith, he said, 'Friend, your sins are forgiven'" .

Faith is imperative for healing us back to normalcy, and removing the aberrations that have been destroying our health. Trust that your Heavenly Father knows best, and pave the way for His plan by devoting your life to righteousness. Faith is the ultimate facilitator for the next step of human consciousness, giving birth to the prolific "Son of Man".

John 3:14-15

"Just as Moses lifted up the snake in the wilderness, so the Son of Man must be lifted up, that everyone who **believes** may have eternal life in him."

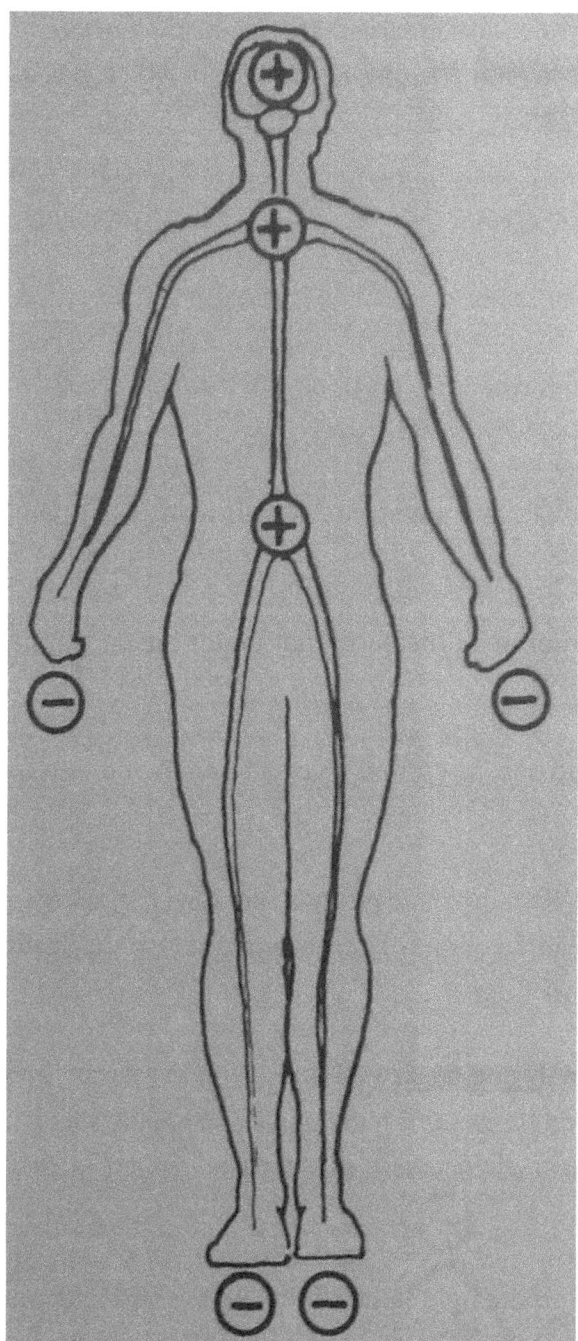

This "snake" is a reference to our spinal cord, which is the redemptive concept of renouncing the primordial sin also perpetuated through the serpentine brain. Along the axis of our nervous system are 7 energy centers, which the Book of Revelation refers to as the 7 seals or the 7 lampstands. These 7 energy centers are also related to the 7 spirits of God, the 7 churches and the 7 colors of the rainbow (part of God's promise). Recently, Neuroscience has been able to locate these energy centers within the nervous system. In Hindu tradition, these are called the 7 chakras.

Dr. Robert Becker incidentally identified the physical basis for the 7 churches which house the 7 Spirits of God. These "seals" are energy centers aligned along the brain and spine. Robert Becker found the scientific substrate for these 7 centers that have been known by mystics and the spiritually adept for millennia. In the spine there are two enlargements (shown as + along the spine in the picture); the cervical enlargement is attributed to the mass of neuronal cell bodies that project to your arms, the lumbar enlargement is a similar mass of neuronal cell bodies that projects to your legs. These enlargements house a significant positive charge in relation to the rest of the spine. These two areas are literally charged, just like the mystics proposed with the chakras. The cervical enlargement anatomically matches the location of the throat chakra, and the lumbar enlargement anatomically matches the location of the solar plexus chakra. At the midpoint between these two locations of the spine is the sinoatrial node of the heart. The sinoatrial node is an independent mass of neuronal bodies that maintains a necessary pace for heart. Although the heart itself is oblique and off-centered, the sinoatrial node is located at the central axis of the spine, in vertical alignment with the cervical and lumbar enlargement. The curvature of the spine allows the sinoatrial node to vertically align with the two enlargements. Becker also found another location of significant positive charge, the cerebral cortex. He found that this positive charge encapsulates the brain, and this is the electrophysiological basis for the crown chakra. In between the crown chakra and the cervical enlargement, aligned in perfect vertical orientation, is the pineal gland. The 3rd eye chakra. The physical substrate which acts as an internal gateway to the spiritual realm.

We are meant to open thee "seals" in order to come to the full expression of God's 7 Spirits, which are also exemplified by the 7 days of Creation.

Revelation 5:1-10

> "And I saw upon the right hand of Him who is sitting upon the throne a scroll, written within and on the back, sealed with seven seals;
>
> and I saw a strong messenger crying with a great voice, `Who is worthy to open the scroll and to loose the seals of it?'
>
> and no one was able in the heaven, nor upon the earth, nor under the earth, to open the scroll, nor to behold it.
>
> And I was weeping much, because no one was found worthy to open and to read the scroll, nor to behold it,
>
> and one of the elders saith to me, `Weep not; lo, overcome did the Lion, who is of the tribe of Judah, the root of David, to open the scroll, and to loose the seven seals of it;
>
> and I saw, and lo, in the midst of the throne, and of the four living creatures, and in the midst of the elders, a Lamb hath stood as it had been slain, having seven horns and seven eyes, which are the Seven Spirits of God, which are sent to all the earth,
>
> and he came and took the scroll out of the right hand of Him who is sitting upon the throne.
>
> And when he took the scroll, the four living creatures and the twenty-four elders fell before the Lamb, having each one harps and golden vials full of perfumes, which are the prayers of the saints,
>
> and they sing a new song, saying, `Worthy art thou to take the scroll, and to open the seals of it, because thou wast slain, and didst redeem us to God in thy blood, out of every tribe, and tongue, and people, and nation,

and didst make us to our God kings and priests, and we shall reign upon the earth.'"

Here it explains how Jesus's sacrifice opened the 7 seals; to open our self to the 7 Spirits of God within us. "The Kingdom of Heaven is within us", ensures us that these are in fact references to bodily structures. Our bodies are transcendental vehicles purposed for the ascent of our soul into the Heavenly Kingdom. This is why Plato compared our world to a receptacle in which souls can mature into the world of Form (heaven). Yet so many of us have gotten caught up with humanly life, which is to sin, and therefore we miss this transformative process into the Kingdom. This can be likened to a caterpillar that is too preoccupied with its life as a caterpillar to ever metamorphose into a butterfly. Instead of ascending our awareness into the 4-dimensional light, we are captivated by the 3-dimensional world.

Baptism: Manifesting Archetype

What is baptism? Many would equate it with the religious ritual of submerging a baby underwater with approval of a pastor. This is the most rudimentary understanding of what it means to be purified through baptism. John the Baptist was known for baptizing people with water, but it is much deeper than that:

Matthew 9:14

>Then John's disciples came and asked him, "How is it that we… fast often, but your disciples do not fast?"

John's baptism involved a complete rejuvenation through water. This involved a water fast, which means to abstain from eating and only drink water.

When the body is in a fasted state, it no longer has to spend energy on digesting food, therefore it can allocate its energy to other parts of the body to facilitate repair and rejuvenation. The blood that resides in vessels near the gut to aid in digestion can now by allocated to other areas of the body to enhance other bodily processes. Water aids in this process because it helps cleanse the body. This is what Jesus was doing for 40 days in the wilderness, he was foregoing a water fast. In 3 of the 4 gospels, Jesus precedes his ministry by being baptized with water, and then entering the wilderness. Here, to show us the path, he purifies himself (not as though he needed purification) through nature. By completely relinquishing material and spiritual possession, the archetypical working of our body and soul is presented.

Jesus was tempted with rulership of the world because this purification process generates hitherto unbelievable abilities. Prior to Jesus this process only involved water purification, but now, Jesus introduces Spirit into the process (John 4:1), which allows the complete process of being "Born Again":

John 3:3-6

>Jesus replied, "Very truly I tell you, no one can see the kingdom of God unless they are born again."
>
>"How can someone be born when they are old?" Nicodemus asked. "Surely they cannot enter a second time into their mother's womb to be born!"

> Jesus answered, "Very truly I tell you, no one can enter the kingdom of God unless they are born of water and the Spirit. Flesh gives birth to flesh, but the Spirit gives birth to spirit."

Baptism has two aspects; John presented purification through water, and Jesus completed the process by introducing Spirit into the process. This spiritual birth is eluding to the Son of Man: the genuine spiritual offspring of the human. He confirms this later in his conversation with Nicodemus:

John 3:13-15

> "No one has ever gone into heaven except the one who came from heaven—the Son of Man. Just as Moses lifted up the snake in the wilderness, so the Son of Man must be lifted up, that everyone who believes may have eternal life in him."

This second birth is facilitated through water and led by Spirit. Genuine Faith in this process is a must. Moses lifted up the fiery brazen serpent in the wilderness. Brazen means unashamed, and fiery is indicative of the flaming sword that guards the tree of life (Genesis 3:24). Therefore Moses was essentially living in a higher plane of being. This is why God gave them "light food" to eat; they were residing in the realm of light, eating the food of the heavens (Psalm 78:24). Anyone who was facing death could look at the brazen serpent **expectedly** and would be cured. So it is with the Son of Man; anyone who is purified materially and spiritually and ventures into the wilderness expecting a visitation from the Son of Man, will undergo a metaphysical change. This is the born again process. Do not believe someone who claims to be born again, but cannot perform miracles. Anyone who is truly born again will be able to do amazing things:

Matthew 17:20-21

> He replied, "… Truly I tell you, if you have faith as small as a mustard seed, you can say to this mountain, 'Move from here to there,' and it will move. Nothing will be impossible for you. This kind does not go out except by prayer and fasting."

This second birth also repairs other parts of the body, which allows it to work to its fullest potential. Remember the parasympathetic nervous system, or the Tree of Life, discussed regarding Adam and Eve? This system becomes fully activated and unleashes the human potential. The parasympathetic nervous system has to divest its energy into digestion, so, when there is no longer digestion required, the other faculties of the parasympathetic nervous system, such as bodily repair, become more active.

When our attention is brought inward, through Divine Insight, we begin to see clearly the Kingdom of God within us, the Son of Man. Through understanding our relation to the God Mind, we can then manifest it on earth. This is when the new dimension presents itself, the spiritual birth, the culmination of the Son of Man. This is the "new heaven and new earth" seen by John, discussed in Revelation 21. Achieving parasympathetic activation requires a complete deactivation of the sympathetic nervous system; removing all responsibility, anxiety, and work that is sin-oriented. Rather, put your complete faith in God, he knows what you need more than you do (Matthew 6:24-34).

"Drop your nets and follow me", says Jesus. This, along with his other teachings, allow us to deactivate our sympathetic nervous system which is activated by fear, anxiety, survival, etc. Few even know that Jesus teaches to not worry about anything beyond the present moment:

Matthew 6:25-34

> "Therefore I tell you, do not worry about your life, what you will eat or drink; or about your body, what you will wear. Is not life more than food, and the body more than clothes? Look at the birds of the air; they do not sow or reap or store away in barns, and yet your heavenly Father feeds them. Are you not much more valuable than they? Can any one of you by worrying add a single hour to your life?
>
> "And why do you worry about clothes? See how the flowers of the field grow. They do not labor or spin. Yet I tell you that not even Solomon in all his splendor was dressed like one of these. If that is how God clothes the grass of the field, which is here today and tomorrow is thrown into the fire, will he not much more clothe you—you of little faith? So do not worry, saying, 'What shall we eat?' or 'What shall we drink?' or 'What shall we wear?' For the pagans run after all these things, and your heavenly Father knows that you need them. But seek first his kingdom and his righteousness, and all these things will be given to

you as well. Therefore do not worry about tomorrow, for tomorrow will worry about itself. Each day has enough trouble of its own."

This passage is a testament to our natural, archetypical ability. This was demonstrated by the patriarchs living hundreds of years as well as the other amazing feats performed in the Old and New Testament. This ability was the norm for humanity at one point.

Truly we have alienated ourselves from our archetypical nature. Our primordial state involved harmonious synchronization with the environment which perpetuated beauty and bliss. Have you ever thought of the consequences of our alienation with nature? We have lost touch with reality, and traded it for a Babylonian nightmare, which is topped with luxury to prevent the slave from realizing his self-induced enthrallment. We put ourselves in slavery as slaves to sin; we are bound by ignorance in a room with an open door which we can exit whenever we follow Jesus's path:

Revelation 3:7-8

> "These are the words of him who is holy and true, who holds the key of David. What he opens no one can shut, and what he shuts no one can open. I know your deeds. See, I have placed before you an open door that no one can shut. I know that you have little strength, yet you have kept my word and have not denied my name."

The reality of nature is transcendental, and we are too distracted with our worldly lives to realize it:

Henry David Thoreau – Walden

> "We now no longer camp as for a night, but have settled down on earth and forgotten heaven."

Jesus discusses this as well, and claims a mere flower surpasses the glory of Solomon:

Matthew 6:28-30

> "See how the flowers of the field grow. They do not labor or spin. Yet I tell you that not even Solomon in all his splendor was dressed like one of these. If that is how God clothes the grass of the field, which is here today and tomorrow is thrown into the fire, will he not much more clothe you—you of little faith?"

Here is a good point. Flowers do not toil to survive. In fact, the human is the only intensive working organism. Think about it. If we omit leisure activities such as eating, exercising, hunting, fishing, etc, then the human by far works the most out of any species. Squirrels do not toil to find nuts, nor does the deer struggle to find grass. It is only humans which have been self-enslaved to our sympathetic nervous system that relies on such an inefficient method for survival. Upon activating the sympathetic nervous system, which is the tree of knowledge of good and evil, Adam and Eve were cursed to work the land:

Genesis 3:23

> "So the Lord God banished him from the Garden of Eden to work the ground from which he had been taken."

Prior to this, they lived harmoniously in the environment living off Divine Sustenance and indefinite bodily repair through a perfect parasympathetic nervous system. Once the sympathetic nervous system was activated, the parasympathetic nervous system could no longer work perfectly, thus giving rise to death and decay; the curse of humankind. Jesus teaches a reversal of this process. The seeker for this transcendental shift must have faith that God will provide:

Matthew 7:7-11

> "Ask and it will be given to you; seek and you will find; knock and the door will be opened to you. For everyone who asks receives; the one who seeks finds; and to the one who knocks, the door will be opened. Which of you, if your son asks for bread, will give him a stone? Or if he asks for a fish, will give him a snake? If you, then, though you are evil, know how to give good gifts to your children, how much more will your Father in heaven give good gifts to those who ask Him!"

Yet so few have known about this secret, and even fewer have acted upon such knowledge. This is important to keep in mind; in terms of seeking your salvation do not let the lives of others deceive you, this is your individual process.

Matthew 7:13-14

> "Enter through the narrow gate. For wide is the gate and broad is the road that leads to destruction, and many enter through it. But small is the gate and narrow the road that leads to life, and only a few find it."

By believing **and acting** upon the Word of Christ, which was epitomized by his life, we undergo a metaphysical change with amazing implications:

John 11:25-26

> Jesus said to her, "I am the resurrection and the life. The one who believes in me will live, even though they die; **and whoever lives by believing in me will never die**. Do you believe this?"

Jesus is not only the resurrection of the dead, but the way of Life for the Living! Those who are alive who follow His guidelines will never die. He means this literally, and expects few to believe these words, which is why he follows the statement by asking "Do you believe this?" This is mind-boggling for anyone newly coming to this knowledge of the infinite. We have been conditioned to think that the only truths in this world are death and taxes, but Jesus died FOR us:

Hebrews 2:9

> "But we see Jesus, who was made a little lower than the angels for the suffering of death, crowned with glory and honor; that he by the grace of God should taste death for every man!"

This is a literal statement. People will say "Jesus died for our sins", but not necessarily know what that means. It means he died as a ransom for our life. He tasted death for every man so that those who follow his Word would elude such suffering. This Love He has for us is amazing. The apostles are exemplars of this notion. After following the Word of Jesus, the apostles reached an elevated state of Being:

Acts 4:31-32

> "After they prayed, the place where they were meeting was shaken. And they were all filled with the Holy Spirit and spoke the word of God boldly. All the believers were **one in heart and mind**."

This is the result of pursuing the Christ Mind. The apostles achieved this state of Mind by believing and acting upon the Word. Because they are of one Mind, everything is disclosed among the metaphysical members of the Mind.

Luke 8:17

"For there is nothing hidden that will not be disclosed, and nothing concealed that will not be known or brought out into the open."

This is a testament to God's omniscience, and also our participation in such an ability. This is why all our actions are accounted for, and also this is why it is imperative you are always seeking to make all your actions perfect, both seen and unseen by others:

Matthew 5:48

"Be perfect, therefore, as your heavenly Father is perfect."

If you want to participate in the infinite potential of the Divine Mind (God), you must become perfect as well. This involves always abiding to truth to the fullest extent. Upon unveiling the Christ Mind (God Mind), Paul attained godly attributes. When the Christian movement was growing after Christ's death and resurrection, the rulers tried to quell the peaceful uprising by making a plot to kill Paul (Acts 23). They vowed not to eat until Paul was dead. Despite their vehemence, they were never able to kill Paul because he was protected by Christhood:

Isaiah 54:17

"…no weapon forged against you will prevail, and you will refute every tongue that accuses you. This is the heritage of the servants of the LORD, and this is their vindication from me," declares the LORD."

Later in Paul's mission, he is even declared a god by those who are observing his incredible power made possible through his accordance to the Word of God:

Acts 28:5-6

"But Paul shook the snake off into the fire and suffered no ill effects. The people expected him to swell up or suddenly fall dead; but after waiting a long time and seeing nothing unusual happen to him, **they changed their minds and said he was a god.**"

These amazing feats were also demonstrated by the saints. There are also a few contemporaries who have been exalted through the power of Christ working within them. Jesus was capable of teaching people to reach the Kingdom within. Other teachers since Christ have had success teaching people to commune with the God Mind, in Christ Consciousness. Never fully rely on the words of anyone who has died, and not subsequently risen from the dead. You should put the burden of seeking Truth on yourself; Jesus's words are your infallible guide. Inside is where the Truth resides.

Now with the veil of ignorance lifted, and the key of knowledge in hand, Jesus's Parables become quite obvious. I'd like to present a parable of my own, which I think sums up our condition quite effectively:

The Caterpillar Allegory – Based on the Children's book: "Chris the Caterpillar"

> Imagine a city of caterpillars. These caterpillars have long forgotten that they are destined to become butterflies. The caterpillars in this city are so enthralled with their lives as caterpillars, that they never take the necessary steps to transcend into the life of a butterfly. Their unnatural creation, the city, has alienated them from their true nature. It has been so long since any caterpillar has been seen to transform into a butterfly, that these caterpillars do not believe their history, and think that it is a mere myth that caterpillars can transform into butterflies. If a caterpillar were to come from nature, and teach the city of caterpillars their true nature, most of the caterpillars would mock the truth expressed by this knowledgeable caterpillar. "Leave behind all my possessions as a caterpillar to become a butterfly? Nonsense!"
>
> The Christ-like caterpillar would explain to these citizens the life of a butterfly and the necessary steps to transform into a butterfly, but this would involve devoting their life as a caterpillar to becoming a butterfly, which most would be too afraid to do. But, those with courage would take the leap of faith and follow the advice of the Christ-like caterpillar. They would transform into the butterfly and fly off into a whole new dimension of being.

Our third-dimensional life is like the caterpillar, and the realm of spirit – the light – is the life of the butterfly. Jesus came to lead us to the light, into the Mind of God. This ascent is exemplified by Paul. In The Acts of the Apostles, we follow Paul's progress as he integrates with the God Mind in Christ. He talks about leaving the ways of the old world and fully embracing the new life in Christ. Paul is presented with the choice of Ascension, which Jesus called the Spiritual Birth:

Philippians 3:12-14

> "Not that I have already obtained all this, or have already arrived at my goal, but I press on to take hold of that for which Christ Jesus took hold of me. Brothers and sisters, I do not consider myself yet to have taken hold of it. But one thing I do: Forgetting what is behind and straining toward what is ahead, I press on toward the goal to win the prize for which God has called me heavenward in Christ Jesus."

As Paul proceeds along the path to Christhood, in the God Mind, he is presented with a dilemma. Should he remain in bodily form and continue to preach the gospel, or complete his ascent to Christ in the light?

Philippians 1:22-26

> "If I am to go on living in the body, this will mean fruitful labor for me. Yet what shall I choose? I do not know! I am torn between the two: I desire to depart and be with Christ, which is better by far; but it is more necessary for you that I remain in the body. Convinced of this, I know that I will remain, and I will continue with all of you for your progress and joy in the faith, so that through my being with you again your boasting in Christ Jesus will abound on account of me."

When Jesus talked like this, the people were confused and thought he meant he was going to kill himself (John 8:22). With the fresh perspective presented thus far, we can now see what Paul and Jesus were saying. In The Father's Mansion, there are many rooms prepared for us (John 14:2). Take a moment to understand what it means to be the Heavenly Father. This means that his children, the Elect, will become heirs to His Kingdom. Upon receiving the Kingdom, nothing will be impossible (Matthew 17:20), as Children of the Most High God (Psalm 82:6). This inheritance is Spiritual, and within us (Luke 17:21).

Romans 8

"Those who live according to the flesh have their minds set on what the flesh desires; but those who live in accordance with the Spirit have their minds set on what the Spirit desires. ⁶ The mind governed by the flesh is death, but the mind governed by the Spirit is life and peace. ⁷ The mind governed by the flesh is hostile to God; it does not submit to God's law, nor can it do so. ⁸ Those who are in the realm of the flesh cannot please God.

⁹ You, however, are not in the realm of the flesh but are in the realm of the Spirit, if indeed the Spirit of God lives in you. And if anyone does not have the Spirit of Christ, they do not belong to Christ. ¹⁰ But if Christ is in you, then even though your body is subject to death because of sin, the Spirit gives life because of righteousness. ¹¹ And if the Spirit of him who raised Jesus from the dead is living in you, he who raised Christ from the dead will also give life to your mortal bodies because of his Spirit who lives in you.

¹² Therefore, brothers and sisters, we have an obligation—but it is not to the flesh, to live according to it. ¹³ For if you live according to the flesh, you will die; but if by the Spirit you put to death the misdeeds of the body, you will live.

¹⁴ For those who are led by the Spirit of God are the children of God. ¹⁵ The Spirit you received does not make you slaves, so that you live in fear again; rather, the Spirit you received brought about your adoption to sonship. And by him we cry, *"Abba,* Father." ¹⁶ The Spirit himself testifies with our spirit that we are God's children. ¹⁷ Now if we are children, then we are heirs—heirs of God and co-heirs with Christ, if indeed we share in his sufferings in order that we may also share in his glory.

¹⁸ I consider that our present sufferings are not worth comparing with the glory that will be revealed in us. **¹⁹ For the creation waits in eager expectation for the children of God to be revealed.**"

John 1:12-13

"Yet to all who did receive him, to those who believed in his name, he gave the right to become children of God— children born not of natural descent, nor of human decision or a husband's will, but born of God."

The commands are simple. Love God, which is easy when you realize He is the Cause of your Life. Glorifying Him is particularly easy to do when you begin to fathom your heavenly Inheritance. Love each other. Have faith in the renewal process, and do not stop seeking until you have found it (Luke 11:9). This is true freedom, Liberation from our life of sin, into a life of endless possibility (Matthew 17:20).

John 8:28-32
> So Jesus said, "When you have lifted up the Son of Man, then you will know that I am he and that I do nothing on my own but speak just what the Father has taught me... If you hold to my teaching, you are really my disciples. **Then you will know the truth, and the truth will set you free.**"

This is true liberation. This Son of Man, our second birth into the world of light. Think of light as the mind of God. Only shadows of the light are subject to time. 3-Dimensional beings are shadows of the light, just like your shadow is a 2-Dimensional representation of your body. Therefore, the goings of your 3-Dimensional life resemble the condition of your spiritual self residing in timeless light. Jesus' teachings allow us to remove the veil of this world, and see our spiritual, eternal life. Our true nature resides in the light. This is why we are children of God and children of the Light. If a child follows the natural path, which is purged of sin, he will inherit his own kingdom of Light which is a branch from Jesus' existence as the metaphysical tree of the multiverse. Our endless potential is described in John 15 when Jesus describes how we are like branches and he is the vine:

John 15
> "I am the true vine, and my Father is the gardener. ²He cuts off every branch in me that bears no fruit, while every branch that does bear fruit he prunes so that it will be even more fruitful. ³You are already clean because of the word I have spoken to you. ⁴Remain in me, as I also remain in you. No branch can bear fruit by itself; it must remain in the vine. Neither can you bear fruit unless you remain in me.
>
> ⁵"I am the vine; you are the branches. If you remain in me and I in you, you will bear much fruit; apart from me you can do nothing. ⁶If you do not remain in me, you are like a branch that is thrown away and withers; such branches are picked up, thrown into the fire and burned. ⁷If you remain in me and my words remain

in you, ask whatever you wish, and it will be done for you. ⁸This is to my Father's glory, that you bear much fruit, showing yourselves to be my disciples."

There is an esoteric term in Latin that says "Solve et Coagula". This translates as "dissolve and coagulate". In our current lives we are like salt, or the coagulate. We are purpose to dissolve into the light of God:

Matthew 5:13-16

> "You are the salt of the earth. But if the salt loses its saltiness, how can it be made salty again? It is no longer good for anything, except to be thrown out and trampled underfoot.
>
> "You are the light of the world. A town built on a hill cannot be hidden. Neither do people light a lamp and put it under a bowl. Instead they put it on its stand, and it gives light to everyone in the house. In the same way, let your light shine before others, that they may see your good deeds and glorify your Father in heaven."

He says we are the salt of the world, and also the light of the world. Light is the dissolved (4D+) state, and salt is the coagulate (3D) state. Just like in the vine allegory where the worthless (sinful) branches are burned, the salt that loses its saltiness (death from sin) is thrown into the fire and burned. This is why we die, because of sin (Romans 5:12). A life of sin means you never fully devoted your life to assimilation with the Christ Mind. But, if we live according to our natural calling, God, we dissolve into the light to commune with the living God

Revelation 22:5

> "and night shall not be there, and they have no need of a lamp and light of a sun, because the Lord God doth give them light, and they shall reign -- to the ages of the ages."

The Word is the light which is the solution receiving the salt. Our dissolution into the solution is the communion with the Kingdom of Heaven; it is our soul tuning into the frequency of light and love. You cannot serve both God and greed, you cannot have one foot in the door. When searching, you cannot look back to the life of old, it will only hinder your progress.

Ephesians 5:8

"For you were once darkness, but now you are light in the Lord. Live as children of light"

John 1:3-14

"...In Jesus was life, and that life was the light of all mankind. The light shines in the darkness, and the darkness has not overcome it.

There was a man sent from God whose name was John. He came as a witness to testify concerning that light, so that through him all might believe. He himself was not the light; he came only as a witness to the light.

The true light that gives light to everyone was coming into the world. He was in the world, and though the world was made through him, the world did not recognize him. He came to that which was his own, but his own did not receive him. Yet to all who did receive him, to those who believed in his name, he gave the right to become children of God— children born not of natural descent, nor of human decision or a husband's will, but born of God.

The Word became flesh and made his dwelling among us. We have seen his glory, the glory of the one and only Son, who came from the Father, full of grace and truth."

The Word becoming flesh is what it means to coagulate, to become salt. The Word, the Light, is the dissolved unified unchanging Form. Jesus became flesh to teach the fellow coagulates, the salt of the earth, how to dissolve into the light. Without the knowledge of the Christ, the salt loses its saltiness and dies. Those who receive this knowledge become children born of God into the Light. For "in Him was life, and that life was the light of all mankind." John the Baptist was not the light, but he observed it, in other words, he observed a glimpse of the light and thus became a witness to the light. At the transfiguration in which Elijah and Moses appeared from the light, they were coagulating, or materializing, from their dissolved state in the light:

Matthew 17:1-3

"After six days Jesus took with him Peter, James and John the brother of James, and led them up a high mountain by themselves. There he was transfigured before them. His face shone like the sun, and his clothes became as white as the light. Just then there appeared before them Moses and Elijah, talking with Jesus."

Here they observed Jesus dissolving into the light, which is why His face began shining like the sun, and his clothes became as light. Moses and Elijah appeared, or materialized, from the Kingdom of Light. This Light Kingdom is what the elect will soon find.

Colossians 1:12

"and giving joyful thanks to the Father, who has qualified you to share in the inheritance of his holy people in the kingdom of light."

This is not as abstract as you may think. The Lorenz Transformation posits that if any material object were to reach the speed of light, it would literally disappear. They demonstrated this experimentally, and showed that as an object approaches the speed of light it begins to contract in the direction of movement. This contraction continues until the speed of light is reached, in which case the object would theoretically vanish. This is not to necessarily say that Elijah, Enoch, Jesus, the ascended masters, integrated with the light by running as fast as the speed of light. Instead, we can understand this idea better through Einstein's famous $E = mc^2$ equation.

$E = mc^2$ means that Energy (light) is equal to mass times the speed of light squared. Do you see what this is saying?! Take a moment to really think on this before continuing. "E" is the dissolved state, and "m" is the material, coagulated state. The conversion factor, or constant, is the speed of light squared. This has been tested extensively, and time and time again the results indicate that $E = mc^2$. This means that all matter, or mass, is super dense light! This is why God's first command was for light to come into existence. With this, He was able to densify the light into any material form that He wanted to manifest through His Word.

This coagulated, materialized state that God created was in direct resemblance of the light, which is why it was deemed to be "Good". God also Crafted sentient, conscious beings from His image (the light). Humans therefore are from the Light, and thus children of Light, seeking their inheritance through righteousness.

The whole earth will once again be covered with the Children of Light. As Children, we grow and mature to become like our Father. He loves us, and intends for us to participate in his ever Loving Glory. Jesus's life teachings show us the way to this inheritance.

John 8:12

"Again, therefore, Jesus spake to them, saying, `I am the light of the world; he who is following me shall not walk in the darkness, but he shall have the **light of the life**.'"

You should seek until you find. Do not become complacent, this process is to be sought during our life:

John 12:36

> "...while ye have the light, believe in the light, that sons of light ye may become."

The apostles came to realize this transformation. They found the true life that coincided with a life fully devoted to the Path of Christ. Please take your time reading this following passage, it has much depth.

1 John 1:1-6

> "That which was from the beginning, which we have heard, which we have seen with our eyes, which we have looked at and our hands have touched—this we proclaim concerning the Word of life. The life appeared; we have seen it and testify to it, and we proclaim to you the eternal life, which was with the Father and has appeared to us. We proclaim to you what we have seen and heard, so that you also may have fellowship with us. And our fellowship is with the Father and with his Son, Jesus Christ. We write this to make our joy complete. This is the message we have heard from him and declare to you: God is light..."

The Bible has been proclaimed so you too can have fellowship with in the Christ Mind. It is your obligation to seek the further mysteries within yourself that are transcendent of this world and adherent to God. A true Christian must renounce his life of old and not look back (Luke 9:62), remember Lot's wife. Remove Pharaoh's influence from your life; no longer will you cling to the world of old due to fear, but rather, you will reborn in the renewal of your mind. Renounce your worldly desires and seek the One who freely gives you Life, for this is the calling of the Cross.

Matthew 19:29

> "And everyone who has given up houses or brothers or sisters or father or mother or children or property, for my sake, will receive a hundred times as much in return and will inherit eternal life."

Amen

www.ingramcontent.com/pod-product-compliance
Lightning Source LLC
Chambersburg PA
CBHW081459040426
42446CB00016B/3310